THE BILLION DOLLAR BYTE

Praise for

THE BILLION DOLLAR BYTE

"Data As An Asset (DAAS) Index—is a digital age innovation that was inspired by my first book One Simple Idea. A few years from now, we might wonder how we managed data without it all these years…Hats off to Justhy for breaking down a complex topic and making sense of it."

—**Stephen M Key**, Inventor, Author of *One Simple Idea Series*

"This is a simple and straightforward writing about Why and How to succeed through Data & People in the Digital Age".

—**Alexandrina Scorbureanu, PhD**, Head of Performance Management for Information & Digital, Assicurazioni Generali Group Hq., Italy

THE
BILLION DOLLAR
BYTE

TURN BIG DATA INTO GOOD PROFITS,
THE DATAPRENEUR® WAY

D. JUSTHY

NEW YORK

NASHVILLE • MELBOURNE • VANCOUVER

THE BILLION DOLLAR B Y T E
TURN BIG DATA INTO GOOD PROFITS, THE DATAPRENEUR® WAY

© 2018 **D. JUSTHY**

Published in New York, New York, by Morgan James Publishing. Morgan James is a trademark of Morgan James, LLC. www.MorganJamesPublishing.com

The Morgan James Speakers Group can bring authors to your live event. For more information or to book an event visit The Morgan James Speakers Group at www.TheMorganJamesSpeakersGroup.com.

ISBN 978-1-68350-428-3 paperback
ISBN 978-1-68350-429-0 eBook
Library of Congress Control Number: 2017901192

Cover Design by:
Rachel Lopez
www.r2cdesign.com

Interior Design by:
Bonnie Bushman
The Whole Caboodle Graphic Design

In an effort to support local communities, raise awareness and funds, Morgan James Publishing donates a percentage of all book sales for the life of each book to Habitat for Humanity Peninsula and Greater Williamsburg.

Get involved today! Visit
www.MorganJamesBuilds.com

TABLE OF CONTENTS

CHAPTER 1

ARE YOU DATA PARTYING LIKE IT'S THE NINETIES OR ARE YOU JUST STUCK?

"I always tell my traders that they would've loved the 1990s because it was a fairly easy time to make money."
—**Steven A. Cohen**, Businessman, Founder of Point72 Asset Management and S.A.C. Capital Advisors

The 1990s were a good time for enterprise technology businesses and IT departments in companies. It was the run-up to the "dot-com era" and preceded our current information revolution by many decades. With the advent of the Internet and the ubiquity of personal computers, businesses could suddenly automate many business processes for the first time.

This was the nascent age of big data, but that term was yet to see widespread adoption. Business didn't always understand the changes that were taking place. We had not planned for, nor anticipated, the age of big data. The closest businesses of the time came to truly understanding big data was through the use of very large databases (VLDB). Companies did not fully understand the relationship between business processes and the data trails they left behind. Few enterprises, especially traditional institutes such as banks and insurance companies, gave data play and say. They didn't take data seriously enough to fully govern its collection and use.

However, companies did understand that they needed to spend on technology and data. For the first time, businesses recognized that information technology provided competitive advantages and they began investing heavily. Billions of dollars started flowing into technology investments. IT departments were flush with cash.

Those were heady, halcyon days for Information Technology (IT) professionals and executives. There was a real sense of excitement around enterprise technologies. Enterprises were implementing many new systems and applications. For large companies, this often meant millions or even billions of dollars in IT spending. Many long-standing companies, which we will refer to as "traditional" or "legacy" companies in this book, were saddled with old systems such as mainframe machines for which they had paid handsomely for decades until that point. The excitement around IT and new emerging technologies was now driving companies to replace these mainframe machines in an effort to move toward a client-server application architecture. At the time, this was novel. Client-server systems would divide tasks and workloads between servers and clients (i.e., service requesters). For these large corporations, this was a massive, and massively expensive, undertaking.

These kinds of massive IT projects were common in the 1990s. As a career starter, an analyst, and a consultant, I worked on many big projects, which were all data or information centric, building management information systems such as data marts, data warehouses, operational data stores, and the like. I helped British Telecom (BT)

Research Laboratories in Ipswich, UK, make the jump from their legacy analog network to a new digital terrestrial network. I was a part of a team that was highly skilled in technology. At that point, I was also simultaneously consulting for Gatwick Airport Limited in London, delivering operational reports for the Operations Director based on a newly implemented client server system. The system was implemented by ICL, UK (which was acquired by Fujitsu). I remember, speeding on the A12 and the M25, leasing a different posh car every time I made a trip from Ipswich to Gatwick. Money did not seem to be an issue either for my clients or me. From a perspective of 2016, these kinds of jobs were expensive; I would say, *very* expensive. In the late 1990s, companies started working with much more data than ever before, updating systems, migrating data, and consuming information in an expensive and time-consuming manner.

These kinds of projects often turned out much larger than they'd first appeared to be. In the late 1990s and early 2000s, One2One—the UK mobile network operator that later became T-Mobile—embarked on the Big Number Change in the enterprise systems. I was leading a team that was responsible for preproduction testing and implementing the massive change in a terabyte-scale data warehouse. I had the luxury of a terabyte-scale database to "play" with. Our objective was to update the data warehouse and the related marts to reflect the national telephone-number format. The change seemed simple on its face; we were making a straightforward change to the numbering system. However, this caused downstream changes in many systems. We had to update over a billion records stored in a major mobile operator's data warehouse. Many more systems were affected. What started off as a simple change started to become a saga. The project ran for over a year!

This may seem excessive, but the executive overseeing the project and his team of consultants were all pleased with our pace. They were happy to give us time. More importantly, they were happy to pay for the investment. They understood that the amount of data was huge and that the investment was a major one. They knew that the great data party of the 1990s was officially *on* and they wanted to be at the party! They were willing to "invest" and *actually* spend accordingly.

This unbridled enthusiasm for all things enterprise information technology made funding IT projects much easier in the 1990s than it often is today. As someone who has been in the industry for close to two decades and who has consulted with numerous large companies in various industries around the world, I can attest that IT departments were not financially pressured and scrutinized in traditional companies the way they often are today. Traditional companies primarily, but not exclusively, formed and came into their own prior to the Digital Age. What makes traditional companies "traditional" is that they do not necessarily utilize digital technology as a "core" function of their business models, nor do they necessarily use digital technology to drive their business processes. Nonetheless, traditional companies were happy to invest and spend in new technology. There was an excitement around new tools and new technologies. Most executives recognized that the tools were getting better and better.

Unfortunately, companies were focused on a specific technology without really understanding that technology. This often led to overinvestment in tools or, put bluntly, just spending for its own sake! IT had become "cool" and the spending spree was on. The world's large legacy companies saw that IT was changing how business got done and they didn't want to be left behind. They invested massively in IT systems to assure that this did not happen. But, without knowing where they should put their money, companies invested in technology somewhat at random. What companies were really buying were not the business tools they needed, but simply shiny new toys for their technologists to play with.

Enter the Digital Natives and the Age of Digital Disruption

Unfortunately, as the pace of technology has increased, legacy businesses have not always kept up.

Let's now fast-forward to 2016. Traditional companies have now been facing decades of industry-wide disruption by new digital companies. These companies, which we will call the Digital Natives, formed in the age of big data.

The defining feature of the Digital Natives is that they are companies that have digital technology as a "core" function within their business models to drive their business processes. Examples of Digital Natives are companies like Google, Amazon.com, Facebook, and other digital companies that have achieved massive financial valuations by leveraging data and emerging technologies that can collect, process, and consume more data faster than ever before. These companies operate under business models specifically designed to capitalize on data and emerging digital technologies.

Traditional companies, on the other hand, didn't arise organically from the age of big data, as the Digital Natives did, but instead, have been reacting to changes in technology and business environments. They are now saddled with legacy systems in which they invested so heavily during the 1990s and earlier.

The cost of replacing these systems can run into the billions of dollars for large transnational companies. A typical enterprise landscape includes a combination of host-based and client-server applications—a near financial, cultural, and technological nightmare to deal with if you are honest, especially if you want to be agile as a business in the Digital Age.

The old technologies, once so shiny and new, have become a liability. The technology and business leaders of many traditional companies feel blindsided. They thought they understood business and technology. Now they find themselves stuck, mired beneath tremendous legacy

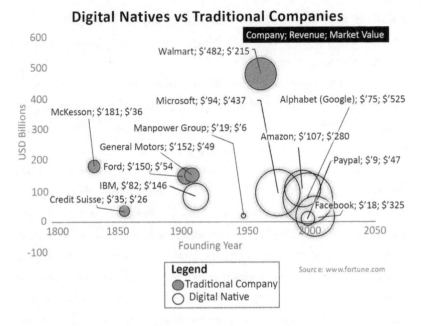

Digital Natives vs Traditional Companies

Company; Revenue; Market Value

Walmart; $'482; $'215

Microsoft; $'94; $'437 — Alphabet (Google); $'75; $'525

McKesson; $'181; $'36

Manpower Group; $'19; $'6

Amazon; $'107; $'280

General Motors; $'152; $'49

Ford; $'150; $'54 — Paypal; $'9; $'47

IBM, $'82; $'146

Credit Suisse; $'35; $'26

Facebook; $'18; $'325

USD Billions

Founding Year

Legend
- Traditional Company
- Digital Native

Source: www.fortune.com

investments in technology that has become outdated. They thought they were still data partying like it was the 1990s, only to realize too late that they are actually just stuck with old systems and applications. They don't know where to go from here. They are being outdone by the Digital Natives, which have achieved valuations ten times that of the most valued traditional companies.

This is happening across the globe. Legacy companies are faltering and even disappearing. According to the American Enterprise Institute, only 12 percent of the Fortune 500 companies of 1955 were still on the list by 2014. A full 88 percent of the top companies of 1955 had gone bankrupt, merged, been bought out, or been dropped from the list by 2014. Only 60 companies remained on the list.

The reason for this is simple: *creative destruction*. The Fortune 500 is churning as new companies take the place of old ones.

Of course, this happens all of the time. Industries shift. Markets collapse. New markets emerge, especially in technology, and eclipse older markets. But what is unique about the last two decades is that whole industries have been digitally disrupted. In today's world, a single Digital Native like Amazon.com, Airbnb, or Facebook, can dominate entire industries, utterly eclipsing traditional companies. The Digital Natives have thus achieved valuations reaching into the hundreds of billions of dollars. They have outcompeted entire industries, upending them in the process.

As shown in the above figure, few traditional companies have valuations even close to the Digital Natives.* Those that are in direct competition with a Digital Native company may find their market share slipping. This is an ongoing process that will not abate. It is no coincidence that 2016 marks both the year that Walmart dropped off the top ten most valuable companies topping the Fortune 500 list and

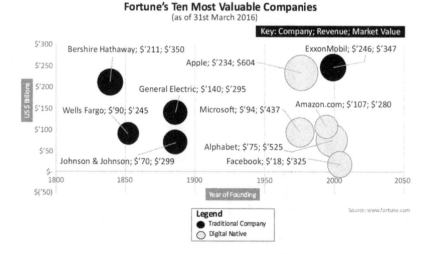

Fortune's Ten Most Valuable Companies
(as of 31st March 2016)

the year that Amazon.com ascended to number nine on the roster. Amazon.com's gain is Walmart's loss. Today, five of the top ten most

---

* As this data changes on a yearly basis, you can find the most up-to-date information at www.thedatastrategylab.com

valuable companies in the world are digital companies, as indicated in the figure below.

Sectors Represented by Fortune's Top Ten Most Valuable Companies Over Last Six Years

2011	2012	2013	2014	2015	2016
Retailing	Energy	Retailing	Retailing	Technology	Technology
Energy	Retailing	Energy	Energy	Technology	Technology
Energy	Retailing	Energy	Energy	Financials	Technology
Energy	Energy	Energy	Financials	Energy	Financials
Financials	Motor Vehicles & Parts	Financials	Technology	Technology	Energy
Industrials	Industrials	Technology	Energy	Financials	Technology
Financials	Financials	Motor Vehicles & Parts	Motor Vehicles & Parts	Energy	Health Care
Motor Vehicles & Parts	Financials	Industrials	Motor Vehicles & Parts	Retailing	Industrials
Financials	Motor Vehicles & Parts	Energy	Industrials	Industrials	Technology
Motor Vehicles & Parts	Technology	Motor Vehicles & Parts	Energy	Technology	Financials

Source: www.fortune.com

The Digital Natives are eclipsing traditional companies because they are adapted to the new business climate. Indeed, they are a product of it. The Digital Natives developed their business models organically in reaction to the new economy. Their business models are fully integrated with their data strategy. They rose to the top by leveraging emerging technologies and big data as part of their core business.

This is not the case with traditional companies, most of which come from the Industrial Age. Many companies are excited about technology, but they still view technology investments as an "expense" rather than a core function and capability of the business model. These legacy companies find themselves clinging to outdated business models that they do not know how to update. They are saddled with legacy IT systems that they do not know how to utilize. They are operating in the Digital Age as if it were the Industrial Age. Technology is no more an enabler only. Today, technology is essential to managing data, which, in turn, is essential for value creation.

It is not that companies do not *want* to change; they simply don't know how to do so. They are scared to abandon the methods and business models that brought them past success. But they *do* want to change. The boards of traditional companies see the success of the Digital Natives and they want in on the new economy. They, too, want to transform their own companies for the Digital Age. They, too, want to enjoy company valuations in the hundreds of billions. They want to leverage technology and data to bring their companies into the Digital Age.

Is the Data Party of the 1990s Still Going or Are You Stuck?

Unfortunately, traditional companies have run into difficulties in trying to replicate the success of the Digital Natives. They face significant hurdles. Traditional companies often lack technical staff with the right skills to leverage data. They may not know how to identify people with the right skill sets, or even how to attract and retain them. Instead, large traditional companies have tens of thousands of "legacy staff" who may not have the right skills for the Digital Age. Traditional companies may even find that their IT employees, who have been maintaining the same mainframe systems for decades, have outdated skill sets.

This puts executives, especially technology leaders, in a difficult situation. Company boards want to embark upon digital transformation programs. They want to invest in big data and emerging technologies like the Digital Natives have. But few boards understand emerging technologies well enough to know what to invest in. They don't necessarily know how a 'data lake' differs from other known data repository patterns, and are very reliant on technology vendors to dictate the direction on which they should embark. They want their companies to attract and retain talent with the relevant digital skills that can help make and implement plans, but no one knows how to get the right people on the bus. They don't even know who the people are or what bus to ride!

The business leaders of traditional companies have not had to contend with these issues before. They do not know how to make the leap into the Digital Age. They must prove to company boards, as the boards themselves must prove, that they can create value in the Digital Age and compete globally and digitally while contending with the burdens of legacy systems and staff, not to mention the complexity of living in a digital world.

As a result of the way companies were data partying in the 1990s, many businesspeople thought that life would be easier by now. They thought technology would make life and business easier. This hasn't materialized. Technology has become complicated and has created fierce competition. Back in the nineties, there were far fewer products and vendors to choose from. Now, there are hundreds of thousands of vendors working in every imaginable area and niche. This level of choice can paralyze company boards and executives. Senior executives are now finding themselves more stressed and overworked than ever. They are struggling to make sense of the changing technology and business landscapes and many are failing to keep up. All the while, the specter of digital disruption from the Digital Natives hangs over them.

Does this sound like you? Are you a CEO heading up a traditional company but struggling to show your board that you can generate much-needed growth in the Digital Age? Are you a new Chief Data Officer, or perhaps a veteran Chief Information Officer, who has to carry the burden of legacy systems while coming to terms with new-age analytic needs? Are you an executive tasked with demonstrating that your business model is still relevant, both globally as well as digitally, when you very much doubt its relevancy? Are you clinging to legacy systems and old business models for fear that your profits and stock shares will slump even further? Are you a CTO going head-to-head with the Digital Natives but realizing that you are on *their* turf and that they have surpassed you despite—or even *because of*—your IT infrastructure?

In short, executives and other business and technology leaders at traditional companies need to start asking themselves, *Are we still "data partying" like it's the 1990s or are we stuck?*

There is a way out for traditional companies. They can identify, recruit, train, and retain people with digital skills. They can learn from, and compete with, the Digital Natives. They can update their legacy systems. They can leverage data for its full value. They can implement emerging technologies. They can update and compete in the Digital Age.

But before any of this can be possible, traditional companies must take a cold, hard look at themselves. If they are no longer investing in data and emerging technologies like they were in the nineties, if they are actually just stuck with their old mainframe systems and other legacy technology, traditional companies must admit they have a problem.

And, most importantly, if they don't want to be the next legacy company to fall victim to the new economy and the Digital Age, they need to do so immediately.

CHAPTER 2

THE DIGITAL ERA AND THE
END OF THE INDUSTRIAL AGE

"I believe that, if managed well, the Fourth Industrial Revolution
can bring a new cultural renaissance, which will make us feel
part of something much larger than ourselves: a true global
civilization. I believe the changes that will sweep through society
can provide a more inclusive, sustainable, and harmonious society.
But it will not come easily."
—**Klaus Schwab**, Founder and Executive Chairman
of the World Economic Forum

The world, and that includes the *business* world, has undergone a Digital Revolution. The changes taking place now are no less significant than those of the Industrial Revolution. Gilles Babinet, the first president of the National Digital Council and author of *L'Ère Numérique, un nouvel âge de l'humanité'*, has described how the mass proliferation of computers started a new Industrial Revolution that is taking us out of the Industrial Age and into the Digital Age.

Computers have been around for a long time, but they are now ubiquitous to every household and business. Computers are everywhere. They are being integrated into our homes, appliances, and vehicles. They touch every aspect of our lives. In the business world, no sector is spared, from agriculture to manufacturing to service. Technology is changing the world. It's an exciting time to be alive, and innovation abounds. This has created a world in which technology can now meet our every need.

The Digital Revolution is closing the distance between people and economies, setting off rapid increases in globalization. For the first time, companies can operate efficiently across national borders. Digitization has made the world more monolithic and interdependent.

One of the results of this digitization is that we now have data on everything. Digital processes leave behind a digital trail in the form of data. Businesses today handle more data than ever before and there are now technologies for parsing and making use of that data profitably. The effect this is having is one of the most profound ways in which emerging technologies are changing government and business.

We have a name for this phenomenon: "big data." Many a book has been written on it, many a lecture given, many a TED Talk gone viral.

But the term "big data" is problematic. For one thing, it conjures up images of Google and Facebook, the kind of digital companies that process five hundred exabytes of data per year—an immense amount of information. In comparison, traditional companies process *petabytes* of data. A traditional global bank in Europe, for example holds about eighty petabytes of data or more. Although this is obviously an order of less magnitude than the data that Google processes, it is still a massive amount of data with great value, which is not always being leveraged for its full value. The business world is now starting to wake up to the immense value of this so-called "small data." Of course, it is only small in relative terms. Traditional companies also have massive amounts of data available to them, which represent a great opportunity if they put this data to use, and a great threat if they fail to do so.

The other reason the term "big data" is problematic is that it places too much emphasis on the data itself. In truth, it isn't the data that has changed. The data life cycle itself hasn't changed over the last few decades. Data is still data; it is just being rapidly industrialized on a massive scale.

Think about the way that McDonald's changed the burger business. They streamlined the manufacturing process so that "billions and billions" could be served. But what they are serving is the same thing: hamburgers—just meat in a bun with pickles and a dollop of ketchup. It's the same situation with data—it hasn't changed, simply the amount that we can process and the level of information and insights that this increased flow of data provides.

What *has* changed are the technologies we use to process and work with data. We can process more data with a higher degree of precision than ever before. We also allow for more complex data, richer analysis, and better use of data, primarily through superior visualization. Analysts can use data in new ways that deliver real enterprise value.

Companies across all industries have been waking up to the fact that emerging digital technologies are revolutionizing business by **creating an asset of data**. There isn't a company on Earth that cannot benefit from increased data and the opportunities it brings. The value of data is certainly not limited to the Digital Natives; traditional companies have just as much to gain from leveraging data as an asset.

Unfortunately, traditional companies have been slow to adapt to the changes of the Digital Age. In my years as a consultant working in data-and-information management, I have seen company after company struggle because they fail to recognize and act upon the opportunity that data and emerging technologies present. They are missing out on one of the greatest opportunities of the Digital Age—a veritable digital gold rush.

But why?

The reason is that many companies, even those with large IT departments, fail to comprehend, organize, manage, and monetize data, and thus they fail to realize its full potential in business. They don't always even understand what data is, in the context of their enterprise.

What Is Data?

Data is simply the trail left behind by business interactions and processes—some internal, and others, external. Businesses all have a business strategy or a business objective, which is translated into a business model. The business model is multifaceted and comprises a number of business processes. Everything the business does is a business process and defines how a business functions. These processes include anything carried out as a normal course of doing business, such as from manufacturing to distribution and everything in between. Stocking a store with inventory is a business process. Selling an item is a business process. Signing a customer into a reward program or promotional campaign is a business process.

These are the same types of processes that businesses have always carried out. The basic structure and function of business hasn't changed much over time. The business goals, models, and processes have always been the cornerstone of business, across all industries and professions. Andrew Carnegie's steel plant had a business model. Henry Ford had a business goal of producing a cheap car that all Americans could afford, which he achieved by creating assembly lines to make this a reality.

This remains true today, even as strategies and models shift and change. Walmart's business model hinges upon a strategy of offering the lowest possible prices, and everything about the way they do business aligns with this strategy. They have processes for acquiring inventory at below-market rates. Their stores are located and set up for efficiency. Even their advertising is aligned with this strategy: "Always Low Prices. *Always.*"

When we say "data" in business, we are traditionally talking about the *structured* data left behind by a business process. Before computerization, this data was either left behind as a paper trail or another non-digital artifact. It was made up of receipts, invoices, ledgers, and any information recorded as part of a business process. With the proliferation of computers, these processes are increasingly digitized. In the Digital Age, these processes always leave behind a *digital* trail of data that is easily accessible. It doesn't end up on paper, locked away in a warehouse somewhere. This also marked the introduction of "unstructured" data, which was not traditionally held in relational databases or repositories. This data is now captured and stored. Companies now have both structured and unstructured data at their disposal, which they can organize, process, utilize, and monetize.

When data trails went digital, our ability to collect and analyze data—and the business processes they represent—improved dramatically. In the Industrial Age, a shopkeeper might only have records of what was sold each day. This data could be used to make decisions about inventory, but it was a matter of intuition and trial and error. In the past, it was difficult to crunch and analyze unstructured data. Auditors struggled to analyze and compute data from a paper trail. Technologists cannot process and analyze paper trails the way they can use available technologies to work with digital data sets today. Just ask the Big Five. The kind of data collection, organizing, processing, and analyzing done by the multinational companies of today simply wasn't possible even a few decades ago.

Efficient mass analysis of data has increased its usability and value. Analytics became possible, which allowed businesses to gain rich insights from data. Technology allowed all of this to be done on the fly, adjusted in real time, which meant that businesses could use data to modify business actions and even aid in carrying out new proactive, and even predictive, decision making. This makes the data you have more useful, as well as more valuable.

Your Industrial Age shopkeeper might only have had data on what was purchased that day, but Walmart and similar companies can track what was bought, who bought it, when it was purchased, whether shelving location mattered, and endless other variables. Walmart can fine tune their business processes around their business strategy. They can also use data to actually carry out new processes, such as matching customers with targeted promotional campaigns. This is why Walmart, who is very good at harnessing data in this way, has become the world's largest brick-and-mortar retailer and, despite pressure from Amazon. com and other online retailers, a successful traditional company. They have done this largely by recognizing the value of data and putting it to full use to adjust their operations.

The Data Deluge

As emerging technologies have increased our ability to process data, it has also increased the amount of data to be processed. The more valuable data becomes, the more of it we create and use.

This is a classic case of the Jevons paradox. In 1865, when the Industrial Revolution was ramping up to new heights, economist William Stanley Jevons noted that the increased efficiency of coal consumption was not leading to less coal being burned, as one might expect, but rather to *more* coal being consumed. With increasing efficiency comes increasing value; of course people would burn more coal! The payoff for doing so was driving industrial growth.

In the Digital Age, we are now seeing the same thing with data. Now that we can process and utilize data with greater efficiency than ever before, that data becomes more valuable and there is a greater demand for it. Data is the coal of the Digital Age and emerging technologies for processing data faster than ever before is the digital "steam engine" driving growth in business data. As the Digital Age continues to unfurl, the world is likely to soon develop a data exchange in which companies can trade data just as they would any other commodity.

The world is literally being inundated with a "data deluge." The International Data Corporation, a market research company working in data, reported that mankind created five exabytes of content between the dawn of civilization and 2003. By 2013 we were creating five exabytes of content every single day. The data we create in a year, if stored on CD-ROMs, would create a stack of CDs that reached well beyond the moon and, within a few short years, beyond the planet Mars. We created 2.8 zettabytes total in 2012, and IDC forecasts forty zettabytes per year by 2020. This is a massive amount of data, increasing exponentially.

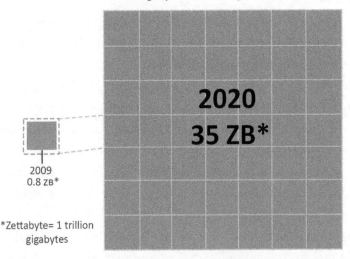

The Digital Universe 2009 – 2020
Growing by a Factor of 44

2020
35 ZB*

2009
0.8 ZB*

*Zettabyte= 1 trillion gigabytes

Source: IDC Digital Universe Study, Sponsored by EMC, May 2010

IDC predicts that it will have increased by a factor of 44 by 2020. One zettabyte is a billion terabytes.

With this exponential growth, we have more data than ever before. We also have *richer* data than ever before. Companies can now track far more than just what is being purchased. They can track its unit rate, whether coupons were used, how placement in the store affects purchases, and so much more. They may be able to identify you by your credit card or a rewards program and actually track your individual purchasing habits. This allows companies to better target ads, coupons, and other materials with microscopic precision.

The data deluge hasn't just meant more raw data. We are also collecting new *types* of data. At the dawn of the Digital Age, most of the data being processed was structured data. This is typically internal data—compiled by companies and stored in databases—that can be analyzed to improve business processes. Now companies also compile and use unstructured data. This can be data about almost anything and everything. External data out in the world is unstructured. It can be measured though and, like structured data, analyzed once it is recorded and organized. But it has to be actively collected. An example of unstructured data is the social media presence of customers or potential customers.

This is new data companies didn't even have access to in the past. For the most part, it didn't exist prior to the nineties, and what information did exist couldn't be easily matched to customers. This has all changed. Wider adoption of digital technologies and increased technological capabilities to measure and collect unstructured data has resulted in access to data sets companies couldn't even have imagined a few short years ago.

Unstructured data has been a boon both for the companies collecting the data and monetizing it (e.g., Facebook, Google, etc.) and for the companies that receive the matched data to improve their processes. In short, it's not just a step up from minor to major league, but a whole new ball game. However, not all traditional companies are ready to hit the field.

How Will Traditional Companies Compete?

The data deluge is changing the world. It's changing business. This creates real challenges for today's companies, but also great opportunity. The Digital Natives are disrupting industries, but there is no reason that traditional companies cannot adapt their same methods and thrive in the Digital Age.

The Digital Natives won't be the only great companies of this century. Legacy companies that are willing to collect data and, when necessary, pivot their business model will also survive and thrive. Amazon.com killed Barnes & Noble, but they haven't killed Walmart. That is because Walmart is well known for utilizing data to adjust their operations. They fully leverage data and they are not afraid to adjust their business model according to their data. They have also made online sales a larger and larger part of their business, even as they continue to focus on brick-and-mortar stores. They have embraced both the Information Revolution and the Digital Revolution.

My advice to traditional companies facing disruption is to become digital companies. This applies to all traditional companies, even those currently in the Fortune 500. All companies will eventually face disruption. There is no industry that the information revolution will not touch.

No company or country can halt this change. You cannot halt the Digital Revolution. You cannot hold back the data deluge. What you *can* do is build a boat and embrace the data tsunami. The successful companies of today and tomorrow, across all industries, are those who not only accept but also *embrace* emerging technologies and new ways of using data. They collect, organize, and monetize data to their competitive advantage.

For proof of this, you need look no further than the companies that are doing this and creating record valuations. The valuations of Digital Natives are often ten times the valuation of traditional large companies. This is because their valuation is based partially on their user base. Typically, more users means more customers, and in turn, more opportunities to capture their interactions and customer journey. This is data. These are the digital trails they leave behind.

This data allows companies to better understand how their customers think and behave, even beyond the confines of how they interact with your business. There is a huge potential for businesses to increase the monetary value of their customer base. Customer data has value. When it is not captured and utilized, that value is wasted. This creates a value around users, whether or not they pay anything. Facebook was valued at $104 billion at the time of IPO. In early 2017, they are valued at approximately $369 billion dollars. This expands with their user base because user data is valuable. According to a report from Appraisal Economics Inc., a Facebook fan could be worth about $174 to a company. Of course, depending on the brand this varies, such as $1613 for BMW fan and $70 for a Coca-Cola fan.

This is a new framework for thinking about data, one that is specific to the Digital Age and a clear break from the Industrial Age. Historically, companies have treated data, and information technology in general, as a cost of doing business. They treated data like garbage that needed to be managed and handled. This could be because many technologists and businesspeople, especially those heading traditional companies, were trained as industrialists. In the technology industry, they are often referred to as "BG"—before Google. They came of age and forged careers in the Industrial Age and that has shaped their worldview. They see data as a raw material that needs to be processed to create a certain output. Data is the input. It goes through processing until it comes out the other end. Data in/data out—that's the industrial mind-set. Data is treated as any other business process.

The problem here is that this mind-set doesn't recognize the *value* or *potential value* of data. Data gets no play and no say, despite its increasing value. What I have seen over and over again in my years working in consulting is that the data in/data out mind-set becomes a garbage in/garbage out mind-set. Why? Because industrialists see data as a cost. It is garbage to be dealt with and processed. They fail to recognize data as the valuable tool and asset that it has become.

The further we get into the Digital Age, the more the industrial mind-set becomes a liability. Embracing the Digital Revolution is not a choice companies get to make. Your best competitors are *already* using data to their advantage and they will eclipse you—and fast. Traditional companies must ask themselves, *Am I keeping up?*

Now that technological advances have torn down geographic boundaries in business, your competitors are competing globally. The global economy has forced faster reaction times in business, and emerging technologies have helped to ratchet up the speed of business. This has made business more competitive and fast-paced than ever before. If you're not keeping up, you're falling behind. Your company cannot afford to tread ground on the same conveyor belt it has been using for the last forty years. Your competitors are turning up the speed. They are inventing faster conveyor belts. They're questioning the entire *premise* of the conveyor belt and looking for whole new ways to do business better.

In this environment, every company operating today must ask themselves these serious questions: *What are we doing to compete? Are we embracing the Digital Age or are we stuck in the Industrial Age? Are we leveraging big data and emerging technologies as well as our competitors? Are we using technology to compete globally? Are we leveraging data for all that it's worth? Do we know what to do with our data and how we need to do it?* In short, *Do we have a data strategy for the Digital Age and is that data strategy aligned with the business strategy?*

For sure, what worked in the Industrial Age won't work in the Digital Age. Chief Executive Officers, Chief Technology Officers, Chief Information Officers, and Chief Data Officers must now steer their companies through the ambiguity and challenges of the Digital Revolution. They have to navigate shifting markets, economic crises, globalization pressures, and new technology that is always evolving. They cannot sit on the sidelines. They cannot adopt the status quo; the old status quo has become dated. They will be put out of business by competitors that are harnessing the value of data. Today, companies doing millions or billions of dollars in revenue stand or fail based on their use, or lack of use, of their data. And yet, data programs and IT departments are often the first to see cuts during tough times.

There are two reasons for this. First, companies think that data programs are too complex and failure-prone. The second reason is that companies don't understand the return they can get on technology spending. It's hard to measure and easy to dismiss. The returns on technology are great, but they are *indirect, as of today* and may seem soft or invisible compared to concrete assets like buildings or machinery.

But in the Digital Age, data matters. Give it play. Give it say. Your best competitors are doing just that. They are not treating data like garbage; they understand that it is an asset.

CHAPTER 3
IF YOU'RE SKEPTICAL ABOUT BIG DATA, YOU'RE NOT ALONE

*"Every person who has mastered a profession
is a skeptic concerning it."*
—**George Bernard Shaw**, Irish Playwright

B ig data" has become a buzzword. The term gets thrown around by the media and business people alike. Newspapers and B2B magazines are full of articles extolling the virtues of big data. We are told that big data is revolutionary, that it will not just change the way we do business, but the way we do *everything*.

Traditional companies see the success of Digital Natives in leveraging big data for even bigger valuations and they want in on the action too. Nevertheless, traditional companies are also hesitant to make huge investments in technology and processes that are outside their current business models. They may dismiss the data strategies adopted by Digital Natives as irrelevant to their traditional businesses, and, in some cases, even too rash and hasty. They fail to comprehend what they could possibly do in order to be more like the digital companies that are, all too often, dominating and disrupting their industries and marketplaces.

In short: traditional companies have had their interests piqued by big data, but they are skeptical and don't understand accurately enough on what they should be spending their money. They cannot tell what is hype and what's not because the digital environment is not one in which they have traditionally operated. They know they should invest, but they most probably don't know where to do so. They don't readily have digital strategies and data strategies to compete in the new digital market. They have to develop new ways of thinking about and investing in data or depend on the big, expensive consulting firms to help make sense of it all. Yet these firms are themselves trying to figure out one technology at a time, NOT one of a company's business processes at a time or one enterprise system at a time, although that's exactly what needs to be done in the first place.

This can be a scary situation for traditional companies. They have been doing things the same way for decades, sometimes centuries. But the fact is that data technologies are changing the way business is done. Emerging technologies are making data more usable and more valuable. It is too great of an opportunity not to invest in. Traditional companies that fail to leverage on the opportunity will lose out to those that do and may even risk elimination.

Traditional companies didn't grow up in the digital environment, but they are operating in it now, whether they like it or not. They must adopt emerging technologies, and they must do so in deliberate and thoughtful ways, considering their legacy constraints. This is a huge transformation effort. It's a cultural change. It's a structural change. It's a new way of doing business. Traditional companies, despite not having the luxury of growing up digital, must make conscious and deliberate changes to the way they use data, and do so rapidly!

This is certainly doable. Traditional companies can have a place at the table, and even enjoy some specific advantages the Digital Natives don't have. However, this is only achievable if, and when, traditional companies start to understand data and how to consume it properly.

Do I Even Need All of These Tools?

Attuned to the buzz, many traditional companies are already making big investments in big data. Research firm IDC predicts that annual spending will reach $48.6 billion in 2019, at a compound annual growth rate of 23 percent. The C-suites of large companies have millions or billions of dollars to invest in IT and, increasingly, they are investing in developing a data strategy. For most executives, this means making investments in new technology tools. They want the "Next Big Thing" they've heard so much about.

This is where they run into problems, with a high probability of failure.

Executives making decisions on technology spending are inundated with options. In all technology markets, including data, there are hundreds of vendors making similar tools to solve similar problems. It can be hard to tell which are better. Company executives often cannot differentiate one from another because vendors create products and services for the marketplace, not for one's specific enterprise. It's the job of the executives—not the vendors—to make them work successfully in their organization.

The C-suites of traditional companies are not adequately equipped to discern hype from real value. They don't have the luxury of time and resources to comprehensively assess their options in order to make decisions about where to allocate IT budgets, what outlays to make, and which tools to acquire and adopt. For the most part, this is done as a reaction to market "chatter," or "qualitative assumptions," at best. There is no scientific and certain method to doing so.

This can make executives very skeptical of not only the tools and technologies, but also of the concept of big data itself, especially if they have been around for a few decades. The market is full of noise and hype. Executives don't know which companies to trust when there are so many vendors, sometimes ones with as big or even bigger company valuations. They don't know which tools to buy because they all look the same but promise more. They have nothing to go on but the word of markets and salespeople. Of course, the techies get excited by the very sound of it. It's both a blessing and a curse, unless you learn how to make it the former.

These decisions can cause paralyzing anxiety for decision makers. Millions—sometimes, billions—of dollars in outlays are on the line. Given this situation, executives become worried and even jaded. Every day there is a new start-up purporting to offer the next big thing in technology. This can make even the most enthusiastic and forward-thinking executives skeptical about the whole endeavor. They begin to wonder how they can ever make an appropriate decision, and simply hope someone they trust can make the decision for them. Which tools are the best? Eventually they may wonder, *Do I need any of this at all? Isn't this just hype?*

The answer is no, it is not all hype.

The truth is that many big-data technology companies are putting out good products. In fact, *most* technology companies that stick around for any period of time are creating good technology offerings. They wouldn't survive the market otherwise. Many of these companies got started in Silicon Valley and are founded and staffed by the best technologists available. Some are even funded by the National Security Agency in the United States. Your data company might well have had a role to play in helping to find Osama bin Laden. These are reputable companies. If you have checked them out, you don't need to worry; they will deliver the goods.

But that doesn't mean that you need *all* of the tools and technologies available in the marketplace.

Big data isn't about tools and technologies alone. It's about how you utilize the data that is relevant to your business model in order to maximize enterprise value exponentially through improved and better business processes. Ultimately, it's all about having a better life on the planet, improving the process of life itself.

Rather than focusing on what tools and technologies to buy from a "shopping list," executives need to pause and ask, *How can data create value for my business?* Only then should they start looking at what tools and technologies to invest in. Most companies will find that they don't need many of the shiny, new products being hawked by start-ups. Many companies will find that they already have quite a few of the tools they need; they just need to be using them in the right ways to create value.

The thing to remember is that big data is still just data; only, it is, as the name implies, data gone *bigger*. Nothing has fundamentally changed in the way we handle data—only the amount of data handled, the variety of data based on the potential sources, and the velocity of data streams that are relevant to the business. These things matter. They allow us to get more value out of data. They open up new possibilities for valuable insights, but the building blocks are the same. The difference is fundamentally one of scale, not type (scale in relative terms depending on your business model).

Imagine you are building a Lego house when suddenly you realize you could piece together more houses and make a Lego city. If you were poorly organized to begin with, more tools will only amplify your inefficiency. On the other hand, if you were well organized and disciplined in the process of sourcing, organizing, and putting the blocks together for building a house, tools will probably make you more efficient and enable you to build a city using similar methods but with better tools. Besides, the multiplication driver is not more tools. For the most part, you just need more blocks—especially if you have been well organized and efficient in the process of building a house to begin with. The process of sourcing the increased number of blocks and organizing them for use, though, now needs to take into account the increased scale, velocity, and probably variety, if appropriate for building a Lego city.

Big data is the same. Companies are still just acquiring, processing, and consuming data—only now there is much, much more of it. Remember that it is a realization that we can do more with our data with currently available tools and technologies.

Companies don't need to look for the latest and greatest thing; they need to look for what works for them. Often, this will be a tool or a technology that is relevant and well understood, and which can be managed within their organization without crippling people.

Companies spend too much time worrying about tools and technologies for acquiring and processing data. The tools one uses are less important than what one achieves with them. Companies need to put the emphasis back on the basics of a process. The data-strategy setup does not need to provide a host of flashy new tools, but it should support the business processes and the business model.

Often—not always, but often—this means sticking with what you know and do. The only difference is doing it *well*.

Cut the CRAP

While this might ease your mind about picking the "wrong" vendor, it probably still won't help you select the "right" one.

With so many good options, which do you choose? What is the best must-have technology? These are the questions company executives are asking themselves. Unfortunately, they are the wrong questions.

Companies don't need to have the latest, greatest technology. Your customers don't reward you for using the latest development in technology. Prospects don't become customers because you used the new, hip data software. Businesses acquire new customers and achieve greater profits when they fulfill customer needs. In business, it's ultimately about serving your customers profitably while creating value for shareholders and society. This is true for all business processes, and data processes are no different. Don't overcomplicate your data strategy by focusing on what new tools you can buy. With small refinements, your old tools might be sufficient to get the job done.

This is because big data is, again, still just data. If you consider the simple value chain of data, it is Acquire, Transform, and Consume. On the supply side, data is treated the same way in any business:

- **Create** the data.
- **Replicate** the data.
- **Append** the data.
- **Process** the data.

Create, replicate, append, process (CRAP)—that's all companies must do on the supply side of data in the Digital Age, regardless of the tools and technologies. In fact, there isn't anything else. This is all there is to data acquisition. Companies the world over adhere to these same steps, and only these steps.

This means that all of the available applications, tools, and services available from vendors serving the data marketplace do one of these four things when reduced down to their actual basic *function*.

The key here is that you need to focus on your business itself and understand what capability is required from the tool or technology. The best way to do this is to first forget about the tools and technologies themselves. Instead, ask yourself what business problems you need the tool or technology to solve. Is it one of cost, one of efficiency, or both? Starting with what tools to buy is putting the cart before the horse when it comes to sound data strategy. You should always first define the problem and then find the tool to address that problem. Let the business needs guide tool selection. Tools and technologies are there to address needs—not the other way around. We don't start out buying a hammer and then look for things to hammer. We make sure the problem is a nail and then we go get a hammer. If the problem turns out to be a screw, the hammer isn't going to be very effective, even if it is the best hammer on the planet!

The tools and technologies available to handle big-data needs are no different. And yet, companies regularly focus on tools and technologies instead of core business needs. More time and resources are spent on selecting tools than on actually understanding and defining business needs. This is because executives are highly influenced by market chatter and noise as opposed to discretion driven from within the organization. The best approach is to just *Cut the CRAP* and figure out what your business needs really are. *Then* you can figure out the best ways to create, replicate, append, and process data based on those particular needs, as far as the supply side of data is concerned.

This allows executives to make decisions about data tools based on what they already know, and what only *they* know best: their core business. Rather than trying to understand a technology bazaar outside their business domain, companies can instead focus on what they actually do as a business. If you're an airport, focus on creating data at the right place. Focus on replicating data from the right place, appending data to the right place, and processing the right data. This isn't about tools; it's about collecting and using the right data.

In the end, the answer to the hype around new technology products is simple: don't buy into the hype. You don't need the latest, greatest, sexiest technology receiving recent buzz from a hype machine. You just need the big-data tools that do what you need them to do, which is to create, replicate, append, and process data. There are plenty of options to choose from and any of them will work; just make sure that they create value.

The key point is to let the business model—not the market or tech trends—guide your decision. This is a much more reasonable thing to ask of the C-suite and a better overall approach to data strategy as well.

Create, replicate, and/or append data; then process it. That's all there is to it. Otherwise, you can cut the CRAP.

Stay with SCRUD

Now that you have moved past Acquire and into Transform, how will you treat your data? How should companies *process* data in the age of big data?

Again, the answer is that data is still data. It is processed in the same ways as before—just at greater volume, variety and velocity.

When it comes to processing data, you may not need new tools. Companies still manage data in the same kinds of relational databases they always have. There is no need to start handling the data in these databases any differently just because you are working with big data.

There are FIVE basic ways in which data is managed and processed:

- **Search** data.
- **Create** data.
- **Read** data.
- **Update** data.
- **Delete** data.

These are the five major functions of persistent storage of data in databases, relational or not. Databases are nothing but dynamic repositories for creating data, reading data, updating data, and deleting irrelevant data. Data has always been handled this way. This is not changing in the Digital Era. Digital Natives still do SCRUD. Big-data vendors do SCRUD. And traditional companies gearing up for the age of big data also need to *Stay with SCRUD*. SCRUD is here to stay; the only difference is that in the future, we will all be doing even more of it, a lot faster.

Unfortunately, technology vendors want to sell their products and services by giving new jazzy names to software with the same basic SCRUD functions in order to differentiate themselves. Don't fall for it. Digital record-keeping methods are the same as they have always been. The only difference is that they can now be performed at scale and a lot quicker. Executives just need to be sure they are managing the right data and leveraging it for value by actually consuming all the relevant data.

Set Your Anchor "VARPP"

After Acquire and Transform, the most valuable part of the value chain is Consume. You might be wondering, *When it comes to big data, where should I put my IT money?*

Let me make it simple for you: stop spending so much money on acquiring and transforming data, and start actually *using* that data. In other words, capturing and integrating data is not as valuable as consuming it. Acquiring and Transforming can be performed by IT services vendors, while your company should be focused on Consumption.

Traditional companies invest too much effort into just processing and repairing data rather than actually using it. They do this because data acquisition and processing are activities they already engage in. They are already part of the business processes. What you need to augment is the consumption of data. Don't just acquire and prep it; *use* it. Meticulously collecting, storing, and prepping data provides no value unless you actually use that data. It does you no good to warehouse dead data; consume it instead.

Data consumption is what traditional companies need to augment most. When it comes to data, companies should focus on:

- Visualizations
- Analytics
- Reporting
- Predictive and Prescriptive Analytics

Visualizations, analytics, reporting, and predictive and prescriptive analytics (VARPP) are how companies actually consume the data that they collect and process. This is the stage at which insights are gained and value is created from data—not the acquisition and processing phases.

In sailing and boating, the warp is the line that attaches a vessel to an anchor, dock, or other vessel. The warp can be used to both keep a vessel anchored in place or to pull it to a new position. When it comes to big data, VARPP can both correctly anchor your company as well as lead you in new directions. You can consume data to validate current business processes, as well as develop new ones that will make capabilities and assets of your data.

VARPP adds value. Visualizations are important because data is abstract. Once the data can be "seen," companies can use it to make better insights. This allows for clearer decision making because executives can actually make sense of the data and what it is telling them about the business.

Reporting is another way in which value can be gained from data. Traditional companies often only do reporting to satisfy regulatory and statutory purposes. It is a matter of compliance and can only be avoided by paying a fine. If this data is not actually used, it becomes dead data stored in a warehouse or database somewhere.

This is a waste. Companies can gain value from the data collected while reporting. They are already required to track this data. They are incurring the costs, so they might as well gain the benefits of the data by actually consuming it. Why treat valuable data as a cost? The data collected by reporting may well be relevant and valuable—but only if you use it.

Analytics are one of the most powerful and valuable uses of data. By enriching data from existing business processes, companies can use analytics to build models to predict future trends and scenarios and make prescriptive business decisions. For example, predictive analytics allow companies to predict consumer behavior, and prescriptive analytics can be used to determine the proper response to that behavior. Obviously, these are insights that add great value, and they should be invested in.

Forget the Hype

Large traditional companies have the ability to spend big on IT and data technologies. They are looking to make significant outlays into big data because they see new Digital Native companies leveraging data for greater revenues and higher valuations. This can create the impression that traditional companies need to invest in "the next big thing." Boardrooms get excited about new tools and technologies, thinking that they will bring their business into the Digital Age. They want the most powerful tools, whether or not they need them. They want the sexiest software that's on B2B magazine covers.

But boardrooms are also skeptical about the whole thing because they don't necessarily recognize that data reflects the business process and they don't know what technologies to bet on or which vendors to trust.

Executives are right to be skeptical and they should avoid hype. At the same time, there is no better investment right now than an investment in data. The volume and variety of data that emerging technologies can process create an unprecedented business advantage for companies looking to go digital.

To summarize, companies must make the right investments. They need to focus on data consumption and not simply acquiring and prepping data for consumption. Data acquisition and transformation are wasted costs unless you invest in consumption. In fact, get the new analytics firms to bid on giving you the best answers using your enterprise data. Without your enterprise data, they may not be as valuable.

Unfortunately, traditional companies often focus too much on data acquisition and data transformation because these processes are already baked into their business models. All businesses with databases engage in CRAP and SCRUD. They're important, they're necessary, but they aren't revolutionary. They won't add new value. They should not be the focus of new investment. What companies need to augment are investments on the consumption of data. Don't just acquire and prep it—*use* it.

Cut the CRAP. Stay with SCRUD. And Set Your Anchor VARPP. Visualization, analytics, reporting, and prescriptive and predictive analytics provide value because they are how we use data. That's something that too many executives of traditional companies don't get. Acquiring data and populating a database does not create value; leveraging data for returns does.

CHAPTER 4

DATA CREATES ENTERPRISE VALUE, NOT JUST JOBS

"Price is what you pay. Value is what you get."
—**Warren Buffett**, American Business Magnate

As I detailed in the previous chapter, emerging technologies have created great business interest in big data. Unfortunately, businesses have primarily focused on the various tools and technologies rather than on data strategy itself. New tools *are* exciting; they allow companies to process and consume more data than ever before and this creates new business possibilities.

Unfortunately, excitement for new tools often overshadows the very purpose of the technology: to use data to create business value. Data isn't about creating new jobs for techies and opportunities to play with the latest and greatest tools. It's about using those tools for business purposes.

But, until recently, data was the purview of techies and the IT department. Traditional companies focused on working with data. They would spend most of their resources on acquiring, transforming, enriching, preparing, and shaping data. Far less effort was put into actually consuming the data. That's because IT departments at traditional companies weren't—and often still aren't—set up to make strategic executive decisions about data. Techies work with data and technology; they don't make business decisions.

The result is that, despite emerging technologies that can make use of data instantly and proactively, data is typically only used to create value during a narrow window of time—only after it is collected and processed. The life cycle of data is spent primarily in the preparation phase, in which it is a cost, not an asset, not a capability, and of no value.

The reasons for this are many, but it is rooted in the fact that it has historically taken a lot of time and effort to get data ready for consumption. Until recently, setting up an enterprise data warehouse typically took about two years on average. That was two years until the data started to provide enterprise value. Data marts take around six months or so to build, but they are typically not enterprise focused; they are more business-process focused. Getting a consistent, enterprise view of data with its life cycle managed optimally, has always been a challenge. But this can change. Data is acquired, transformed, used, and archived. With technology available today, value can be derived much earlier and for longer in the life cycle, even if it is purged and archived. Traditional companies spend an inordinate amount of resources on processing data, without adequately managing its life cycle for value creation.

To operate effectively in the Digital Age, traditional companies need to extend the life cycle of data in order to extract maximum value from it. Data needs to start working sooner—immediately, where possible—and remain in use longer. This is made possible by emerging technologies. Data can now provide value from the moment it is created to after it is archived, whereas in the past, data was dead as soon as it was archived.

In 2015, I visited the scanning center of a Fortune 500 global bank where I was consulting. They were scanning documents and then sending them straight to storage without keeping them available for further analytics. The document trail was a rich source of valuable insights and analytics of the customer engagement and contact processes, which could have been of huge benefit.

Unfortunately, there was no investment made to convert this information into analytics. It was just preserved for regulatory purposes. The data was a sunk cost. The company was putting huge amounts of resources into organizing this data, but not using it. What a waste! They might as well have buried the data instead. They could have held a funeral since, unused, the data was thoroughly dead. The cost of a funeral would actually have been lower than the cost of storing all of that dead data.

This was, and is still, the traditional way of doing things. However, new emerging technologies can now scan archived document trails and extract unstructured data that would have previously been unavailable. This data can be used for rich analytics, extending the life cycle of the data and getting more business value out of it for a longer period of time.

With the Right Technologies, Enterprise Data Provides Enterprise Value

I worked on a data-warehousing project for T-Mobile back when they were still operating as Mercury One2One. It was 1998 and the early stages of mobile telecommunications. Our team helped build and operate a world-class data-warehousing system for the company. It was something we could be proud of, but we failed in a very typical way: we failed to set up the data warehouse to fully monetize the company's data holdings. This is a classic oversight of traditional companies, both then and now.

This doesn't happen with Digital Native companies. They developed and mastered modern data monetization. Amongst the Digital Native companies, Google spearheaded innovative ways of monetizing data through advertisement revenues.

Google is not a technology company so much as a digital advertising company. Google processes a billion search results per day, offering billions of ads alongside each one. Approximately 95 percent of Google's revenue comes from advertising, and roughly 70 percent of all advertising revenue comes from Google AdWords, which allows advertisers to buy ad space at the top of relevant Google searches. They also sell contextual advertisements targeted at viewers based on data-related heuristics under Google AdSense. Both of these programs monetize Google's data while generating even more user data. They were innovative at the time they were rolled out, and were part of a culture that recognized data as an asset.

Google and the other Digital Natives have realized success that traditional companies need to emulate. That starts by recognizing that data is inherently valuable and treating it appropriately. This isn't just for Silicon Valley companies. It isn't just about creating more jobs for techies. It's about bringing traditional companies into the Digital Age by treating data as an asset.

Successful traditional companies are doing just that. They are using data to adapt to the changing business landscape. Again, consider T-Mobile. The data warehouse was a key repository to capture customer-centric data. The industry was going through major shifts in the late 1990s and early 2000s. The importance of voice was diminishing and non-voice content was becoming more important. This data revealed that networks and service plans had far less impact on buying decisions than devices and applications. This meant that networks and service plans wouldn't bring in new users unless they offered extremely good service packages. Significant investments were made into 3G and UMTS in order to provide more value to this new breed of mobile user. Today, there are numerous price plans offered by mobile-phone operators.

The key takeaway here is that, even as the industry changed, data retained its value and allowed the telecom companies to make informed decisions based on high-quality insights. Telecom companies were thus able to transition with the market. In the case of T-Mobile, this was facilitated by a well-organized, well-structured, customer-centric enterprise data warehouse. Data repositories that were once just data warehouses became what are now known as "customer-centric" or "person centric" data stores or repositories or hubs. The data they store allows companies to better understand markets and customers. That's what this is all about.

Furthermore, data retains its value over time—even in the face of massive industry shifts—if it is well organized and structured for consumption.

Maximizing Your Data Assets

Optimizing the data life cycle and maintaining well-structured relevant data are key to getting more value out of data. Companies can reduce sunk costs, recapture lost value, and generate new revenue and capabilities by making use of emerging technologies supported by a sound data strategy that values data and handles it appropriately as to maximize its life cycle and utility.

There are at least five steps, or "rules," for doing just that:

1. Build Rules for Inbound Data.

Data has no value unless it is relevant to the business model. Companies need rules and protocols that ensure they collect the right data. Creating rules around inbound data that allow you to collect more data, and more relevant data, increases the value of your data sets.

Companies often miss relevant data because they don't have rules in place to collect it. This is common with data not collected in the normal course of business. Many traditional companies capture data by default as part of necessary business processes and compliance. Companies often try to solve problems with their data without questioning whether they have all of the data. You cannot just look at the data you have on hand; you have to consider what other data might exist. This means looking beyond the structured data collected during business into possible sources of relevant external data.

For example, booksellers can gain extra value from data beyond that collected from their current customers. There are readers who are not in a seller's current customer base. By looking for external sources of data, such as reviews from Goodreads and Amazon.com, booksellers can glean insights into the habits of *potential* new customers.

And readers aren't the only source of relevant data in this case. Data related to publishers, printers, book vendors, and the whole publishing industry is also relevant to booksellers. This data is often not internal data, and booksellers have to go out and actively collect it. That only happens with the right rules in place for doing so.

This is a proactive approach to data. Most traditional companies take a reactionary approach instead because they have always seen data as a cost of doing business, not an asset. They collect only the data they need to collect for regulatory and business reasons. The value of this data is often limited because it is only used to meet a limited set of requirements or regulatory compliance. There is likely to be other relevant data that tells a more complete story, but without the right rules in place, companies will never see this data. It's not considered a requirement, although it is actually relevant to the business model.

By setting rules around inbound data, companies will be better able to capture more data relevant to the business model. This is key. You need all of the data you can get, not just what's at your fingertips. Don't stop with the data you have on hand. Collect all data that is relevant to your enterprise business model.

Understand the wider context in which your business operates and ask yourself, *What data am I missing?* There may be more data sources of high-quality relevant data than you currently realize.

2. Create Effective Performance Reports in Order to Manage and Control Data Assets.

Companies need relevant data flowing into the organization in order to be able to consume it. The key word here is "consume." Data that isn't actually used is a cost and provides no value. Data that performs no function has no value.

In order to ensure you're getting your money's worth with your data, you cannot just track data. You must also track its actual performance, use, and value. Companies must know exactly how data contributes to the business processes and the business model. You have to know what your data is worth, and why. This requires careful reporting and handling of data management. For example, when a prospect becomes a customer, the value of his or her data goes up. This changes the role of their data, and it must be managed appropriately in order to get the full and correct value out of it.

Set up standardized methodologies for tracking the role data actually plays. Create effective performance reports that allow you to better manage and control data assets. It's not enough to keep records; you have to know why you're keeping them and what role they play.

3. Comply with Official Regulations in
Order to be Relevant in the Digital World.

Every industry has its own set of compliance rules. Some are more regulated than others, but they all have regulations. The financial industry has copious regulations surrounding financial institutes that have been in place since well before the Dodd–Frank Act complicated things further. Insurance must comply with the Solvency II Directive. Telecommunication companies must comply with the Ofcom Broadcasting Code. US health-care organizations comply with HIPAA, and much more.

Compliance is a necessary evil. Organizations and companies must adhere to their respective set of rules and regulations in order to operate legally. This can take substantial resources depending on the size of the organization and the areas of operation. This is especially true for large corporations operating globally, where they must contend with different compliance rules everywhere they operate.

Large organizations must manage compliance efficiently in order to operate globally. This is as much a science as an art. Often compliance is so complicated that companies will just ignore regulations and deal with them by paying fines. This is probably not the best way to handle the situation. It is better to make sure you are handling compliance efficiently and using the data collected for compliance to also create enterprise value.

Ensure that you have standardized mechanisms and protocols for handling compliance in order to keep costs down and efficiency up. Do not waste the data you have gathered. Just because data is gathered for a regulatory purpose does not mean you cannot consume it for growth purposes.

There's no reason not to do this; if you're already collecting it for the regulator, why not also put it to use in the business? This data is often overlooked because its primary function is to meet regulations—but much of that data will be relevant and have real business value.

4. Understand a World toward Standards Breeds Governance.

The term "governance," as used commonly in business parlance, means next to nothing. The term is an abstraction and, all too often, the abstraction of governance on paper and in the boardroom has little to do with how things play out on the ground. This kind of poor governance breeds infighting within an organization.

Don't let your governance become a liability. Governance must be based in standards and those standards should be value based. In the case of data assets, which have so much value, this is doubly important. Directives and internal rules should be judged on how they contribute to the bottom line. Governance should never exist for its own sake. It must add true enterprise value, in actual dollar terms, or the organization is simply making rules to justify the role of the rule makers. Rules that don't add value merely create costs by hobbling an organization.

Value-based governance should be implemented at every level. Don't fall victim to legacy governance. Businesses often operate in certain ways simply because that's how things have always been done. This is never a good reason, and in a world where technology and regulation change so fast, companies today can quickly find themselves operating under yesterday's policy assumptions unless they update continuously.

For example, data security at traditional financial institutions is typically handled by securing data at the perimeter. This doesn't make sense today. As business models in the digital world are more interdependent than before, there is an inherent need to create interfaces of data exchange between enterprises, sometimes across numerous countries—and even continents—with varied security and legal needs. Security has to be structured appropriately in order to extract maximum value.

This is especially true of data because it has so much inherent value. For example, financial institutions with a large customer base should make use of the rich data available on online forums and social media websites. But this external data requires an exchange capability to utilize data from outside of the organization. Traditional companies rarely assimilate this data into the company, but with appropriate rules, data exchange capability with an appropriate security model can add maximum value.

Companies need the right rules in place for engaging with enterprise data. They need rules to govern how data is organized, stored, processed, consumed, and otherwise handled. The right way to govern data is always the way in which maximum value can be realized.

5. Raise the Priority of Data That Creates New Wealth and Opportunities—Not Dead Data.

Knowing the value of your data allows companies to place greatest priority on data that creates new wealth and opportunities for the company. Companies should prioritize this data and organize their data in a way that does so. Traditional companies often waste resources working with dead data, such as data purely focused on governance, because there are already processes in place for working with this data.

The data companies have on hand is not always, or even usually, the most valuable data. Increasingly, it is the combination of internal and external data that holds the most value because it is this enriched data that creates the most insights and thus, the most opportunities. External data can lead to new customer insights and business opportunities. Internal data is likely to be related to existing customers and processes. This data has value, but unless relevantly enriched with appropriate data, it is less likely to present new opportunities. New opportunities and new customers often mean new dollars coming into the organization. This is growth.

Data Is of Board-Level Importance

As large traditional companies wake up to the age of big data, data strategy has become a matter of boardroom-level importance. Today's boardrooms take data strategy every bit as seriously as business strategy. This was never the case before. Traditional companies are seeing the Digital Native companies racking up massive valuations, ten times that achieved by the most successful traditional companies, and they're doing it with data.

Traditional companies want in on the action. Increasingly, traditional companies are developing digital business models in the boardroom. They understand data technologies can no longer be ignored, and that means integrating them into the business model. Failure to do so means ultimate failure. Since the 1950s, 88 percent of Fortune 500 companies have disappeared. This is because they fail to remain relevant as the business environment changes. In many cases, these companies thrived in the Industrial Age but failed in the Digital Age. Companies and boards that lack the capability or capacity to make use of big data and analytics are being left behind. More will fail until the last men standing are the Digital Natives and the traditional companies that went digital.

Traditional companies don't necessarily need to become digital companies, but they should be relevant in the Digital Age. A traditional bank is unlikely to ever look like Twitter, but today, they all offer online banking. Some, such as Capital One, offer fully online services and don't operate many, if any, physical banks—only ATMs, kiosks, and robust digital offerings.

All of this online activity creates new data trails that are assets. Ignoring data is ignoring assets. Boards wouldn't dare ignore other assets that can increase shareholder returns—so why keep ignoring data?

The big decisions around company data cannot be made by company techies. There are executive-level decisions to be made about how to allocate resources, build up technology capabilities, and compete in a Digital Age. Traditional companies have to make investments in analytics, and make this part of their business processes. This must be done from the top; it cannot be left to the techies in the IT department. The people who use the emerging technologies are great at their jobs, but the boardroom is where executive-level decisions are made.

Boardrooms need to do at least three things that techies cannot do in order to use data to return greater value to shareholders. First, they need to extend the life cycle of the data value chain. Traditionally, data consumption and reporting were the last stage of the data value chain. Companies would collect data, process it, and only then use it for value-generating reporting and analytics. This paradigm no longer works. Emerging technologies allow companies to derive value from data at every stage of the life cycle. Companies today need to start utilizing and consuming data from the moment it is created to long after it is archived.

For example, companies should now start utilizing social media data the very instant that it is generated. The data can be used in real time to create value by adjusting pricing, giving targeted promotional offers, and even realigning the social media campaign itself. The data can be used as a capability to offer better services. Consider how Uber uses surge pricing to bring more drivers to underserved areas. Traditional companies can do the same type of things with their data without having to go entirely digital.

The second thing boardrooms must do is oversee the use of big-data technologies in auditing. Auditing is complicated and resource intensive. Large companies may spend several months per year struggling to complete internal and external audits. Data technologies can make auditing easier and more efficient, mitigate risk surrounding auditing, and create new value by better utilizing business process data for auditing. This is because new technologies allow companies to better see what's going on and unlock new insights into the auditing process and the information gleaned from it.

The third responsibility boards have regarding data is to ensure that data is producing maximum value for shareholders. This is literally the role of companies, as board members are required to return value to shareholders above all else. Failure to use data to do so is a failure of their first duty. Data can unlock new capabilities and be leveraged as an asset to create value for shareholders. Many companies already do this, but it can be done to a much greater degree, especially by traditional companies with legacy cultures. The Digital Natives had the advantage of growing up in a digital environment; their processes were adapted to the environment. Traditional companies didn't have this luxury. They have to be active in creating new rules, culture, and processes that bring their companies into the Digital Age. They were not born adapted to the environment, but they must become so now.

For this to happen, boards must take on a greater role regarding data and be proactive in developing their data strategy. Previously, companies made reactionary decisions about data. They used reports, which might have been months or even years out of date, to make decisions about future actions. This is outmoded and even irresponsible to an extent. New technologies allow data to be used in "real and right" time, and it must be managed as such.

Things move so fast now that boardrooms can start to feel like *boiler* rooms. It is only by using data as a capability and asset, with the help of emerging technologies, that boards can keep up. There is no other way to assimilate, process, and make sense of data in real time. Traditional companies have never before had to operate in this way. The transition can only be made if boards take an *active* role. This isn't a job for the techies; it's a job for the C-suite.

CHAPTER 5

DATA STRATEGY: DATA ASSETS ARE BETTER THAN DATA LIABILITIES

"Sound strategy starts with having the right goal."
—**Michael Porter**, Economist, Harvard Business School

To compete in the Digital Age, a company's data strategy must be central to its business strategy. Companies need a data strategy that is appropriate to the Digital Age, meaning that it reflects the true and full value of data and all of the ways it can return enterprise value.

Data can, and should, mature within companies in three ways as part of the Three-Step Data Maturity Mantra, as depicted in the data strategy blueprint figure below:

- Data Serves the Purpose
- Data As A Capability
- Data As An Asset

These are *not* mutually exclusive and should, in fact, always be executed in concert. Think of them as a ladder that enterprises must climb in order to extract the full value of available data.

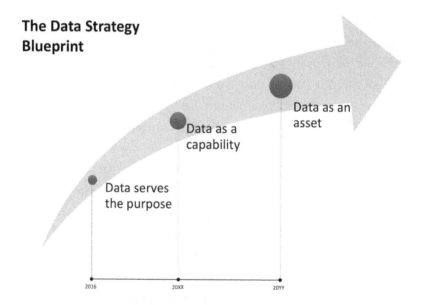

The Data Strategy Blueprint

Data Serves The Purpose

This is the traditional way of thinking about structured data. Companies collect and analyze the data trail left behind by basic business processes. Generally, if the data is there and the business processes are executing as expected, everyone is happy.

Most large traditional companies are working with legacy systems that hold legacy data, which may date back as far as the 1970s. Digital Natives, e.g., LinkedIn, Google, and Facebook, do not have this problem. This data exists in structures and formats that cannot easily be parsed and analyzed by today's available technologies. This means that companies cannot easily access, transform, or analyze the data without first preparing the data for these new insights. It wasn't stored to be used the way we use data today. Just making sense of the data might take months.

All of that internal structured data was typically not stored with any unstructured data. If a traditional company tracked unstructured data at all, they kept it in a separate large-scale system containing scanned documents of various types. This system was separate from the rest of the data. There is no way to integrate these two systems without first reorganizing the data so that it is accessible, integrated, and provides rich and meaningful insights about value.

Without taking the steps required to do that, a company will find that the data is merely *serving its original intended purpose*. This does create value, but it's not a capability or an asset. The data is doing what it was designed to do, but it's not doing anything more. However, with today's technology it *could* be doing more, and a company's failure to utilize this technology results in uncaptured value.

But, in its current state, such data cannot be used without months of data preparation. This is highly inefficient and can severely constrain a company's capabilities for as long as it runs programs to do this. I have seen companies run their data departments this way for *years*.

Data As A Capability

Spending months to make data usable every time you need to use it limits its value. But there is an answer: data can be restructured and migrated to systems that allow for easy, timely and even immediate access.

Improving technology has allowed many companies to do just this. They are restructuring their data so that it can better serve the needs of the enterprise. The data trails left behind by businesses processes, formerly merely collected, reported and maybe analyzed to the best possible extent, is often now being restructured to be more useful to the company. It is accessible on the fly, making it useful in carrying out and driving business processes, rather than merely reporting about them.

This allows for new capabilities. Data not being made to serve the company is data just for the sake of data. It's serving its purpose, but it's not being put to maximum use. But once data is properly structured and organized, it can be used in ways that extend beyond its original intended purpose.

Consider the case of an organization that undergoes annual internal and external audits. In the past, this would have been an exercise in decoding "paper trails" and "transactional trails" left behind by the business processes. It is not normally easy to analyze. But if the data is organized and stored in a way that makes possible reporting back to auditors, regulators, company boards, owners and investors, and customers in an efficient, sustainable, and profitable manner, the company has graduated to using data as a capability. Data no longer exists only for its own sake. It now has something to contribute to the organization, as opposed to just taking up storage space.

When companies use data as a capability, they will find themselves in a place where:

- The business strategy is well understood by the enterprise.
- Business processes are well defined and reasonably disciplined, but not fully automated.
- Business processes have clear ownerships.
- Data has clear ownership and is well catalogued for internal use.
- Data is valued within the organization.
- Organizational culture is more results oriented.

- There is evidence of a structured delivery capability within the organization that is using data and information.
- Innovation becomes a possibility.

Data As An Asset

Data won't reach its full value until that value is recognized and monetized. This is the mark of today's successful digital companies. When companies graduate to this level, they do more than use data as a way to carry out its purpose or as a capability. They treat data like the asset that it is. Data is used to drive revenue and profits *directly*.

My bet is that this is the future of all business. Data has intrinsic value that can be leveraged and even sold. Data is becoming a precious, tradable commodity.

Many Digital Native companies have already made this their business model. Facebook, LinkedIn, Twitter—these companies aren't just social media companies. Their business is in data. They have attained astronomical valuations by expanding their user base and thus increasing the amount of data they hold. Google isn't valued at half a trillion dollars because of its search engine and e-mail service. These features are free. The valuation comes from the extremely rich data collected from its vast user base, which can be monetized through advertising and other methods.

If you think this only matters for the likes of Google and Facebook, think again. All companies operating in the Digital Age must take advantage of opportunities to leverage data for higher profits. Data is valuable in all industries, meaning that it can be used to make money. More revenue makes companies more competitive; it's as simple as that.

When companies treat data as an asset, they will reach a place where:

- The business strategy is well understood by the enterprise.
- Business processes are well defined, disciplined, and efficient, and high levels of automation exist.
- The organization is data centric as well as person centric.
- Data has clear ownership and is managed as an asset *with actual monetization.*
- There is an understanding in the organization that data is an asset.
- Organizational culture is more purpose oriented.
- There is a higher maturity of delivery capabilities in the organization using data and information.
- Innovation is *constant.*

A Three-Pronged Data Strategy for Today's Digital Enterprises

To better understand how companies can use data in these different ways, let's consider a real-world example. Early in my career, I worked as a consultant for a large London airport. My job was to analyze the efficiency of a passenger aircraft stand. I was supposed to extract data from an operational system and compute the efficiency of airport stands at the gate.

The Director of Operations wanted to analyze how efficiently aircraft stands were being used in the airport in order to allocate them properly. This is a classic case of *data serving its purpose.* The airport wanted to collect and analyze data in order to better allocate stands to handle departures and arrivals more efficiently. This was a value-added endeavor, but it took months of analyzing the data to put out a report that the airport could use to improve its business processes.

This is all well and good, but with today's technology, the airport could do so much more. There is no reason why the status of the stand cannot be made available to operators in real time. If the data is structured in the right way, this can be automated. Algorithms could even predict which stands are most likely to be available or unavailable. This is what it means to use *data as a capability*. The airport could use technology in service of its business processes. This is data that is maturing to enterprise value!

Of course, the true holy grail of data strategy is to use data to create true economic value. If the airport uses data about an underutilized stand to offer a discount to their customers i.e., airline operators thereby increasing their traffic which in turn converts to airport revenue, they have just used the data to earn more money. Whenever companies sell data or use it in a way that directly drives higher revenues, greater profits, or larger market share—and ultimately a higher return to shareholders and other stakeholders—they are using data as the asset that it is.

I want to stress that all three of these strategies are important to getting the most out of your data. This book privileges using data as an asset only because so few companies actually use data in this way. Most top companies use data to serve its purpose. Many even use data as a capability. But in my years of consulting with companies on data strategy, what has become apparent again and again is that what sets the best digital companies apart from the rest is that they treat data as more than just data. They also consistently utilize it as a *capability* and an *asset*.

In short, companies with effective digital strategies recognize and realize the full and complete value of their data. They may do this by following the Three-Step Data Mantra.

CHAPTER 6

HOW DATA INTERSECTS WITH YOUR BUSINESS MODEL AND BUSINESS STRATEGY

"You can have data without information,
but you cannot have information without data."
—**Daniel Keys Moran**, Programmer and Science Fiction Writer

T he world has entered a new era of computing in which the pace of business moves faster than ever known before to this generation. Consumers, clients, companies, and indeed, the whole economy, have become faster paced, less predictable, and more volatile. This is the new normal. This fast pace of business is producing more data than ever before. Often it is more data than traditional companies can keep up with considering their "traditional" business model.

This wealth of data is the result of new business models that are innovative by design, complemented by massive leaps in technology advancements, which, for the most part, seem disruptive to the traditional business. The Internet of Things has resulted in data flowing from new sources. Data no longer comes just from computers, but also from phones, cars, transit use, health monitors, home appliances, credit card machines, monitors, and *much* more.

Such gains in data can allow new insights that enable companies to better understand and engage with customers. This ultimately drives new business opportunities and generates new business value.

There are other emerging technologies as well that are leading to more enterprise data. For example, cognitive computing systems use machine-learning techniques to help companies make better sense of the world. These systems actually get "smarter" and better the more they are used, producing more data of ever-increasing quality. This allows companies to derive better predictions and analytics in order to outthink their competition.

New data is also being generated not just by devices, but also by the practices that have arisen around them. Businesses are partnering in new ways, such as by creating application programming interfaces (APIs) that allow companies to take advantage of shared data. Collaboration means that companies have access to more shared data as a part of their business processes.

The IoT, the API economy, and cognitive computing are just three trends that are changing the business and information technology ecosystem. Combined, they are helping IT leaders master digital transformation through greater business intelligence than companies have ever had access to before. This has largely been the purview of new digital companies at the vanguard of the digital economy.

The problem for traditional companies is that they are now tasked with keeping pace in order to survive, leave alone thrive. They are struggling to keep up with the rapidity of this change. Their business models are traditional in nature. The enterprise technology strategies, business processes, data strategies, and cultures are of a traditional mind-set. They have inherited legacy business models and have evolved this far into the Digital Age through the Information Technology Revolution of the 1990s. But, can they survive with the same strategies that got them here to begin with? Digital Native companies, on the other hand, have the luxury of successful strategies related to technology, data, as well as business processes that are part of their core business models that are apt and perfectly suited for a digital business model of the Digital Age. They are well set to create massive economic value as compared to their traditional peers.

Traditional companies are now under pressure. They must catch up with the Digital Native companies that are disrupting their industries. To do this, traditional companies must be nimble. They must be flexible. But, above all, they need to develop data and technology strategies that can withstand frequent and rapid change to the business ecosystem. These changes in the business ecosystem necessitate quick changes to the business model. Therefore, allowing them to adapt to "techtonic" shifts in their respective sectors.

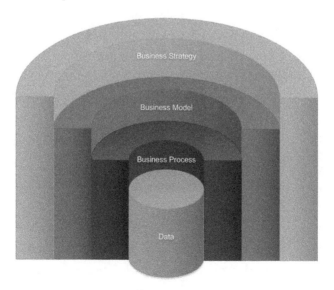

How Data Intersects With Your Business Model And Business Strategy

Digital Disruption Is Here to Stay

For companies operating in the Digital Age, disruption is the name of the game. Digital Natives are benefiting by being early adopters of digital strategies. They have business models that arose organically and have allowed them to reach valuations never seen before.

For traditional companies, the situation has never been bleaker. Once stalwart companies now face extinction. They are operating under outmoded business models that fail to harness emerging technologies that allow better digital and data strategies. New digital competitors are mopping the floor with them.

Examples are not hard to find. Airbnb is cutting into hotel profits. Uber and Lyft are undercutting the taxi industry. Amazon.com long ago disrupted the retail market that Walmart and Target worked so hard to capture in previous decades. Companies like eBay and Craigslist disrupted the classifieds, cutting into newspaper profits and undermining traditional journalism. Newspapers and magazines have folded en masse, while digital journalism sites, like BuzzFeed, that focus on "viral content" have enjoyed tremendous success. Blockbuster is gone thanks to Netflix and Hulu. This list goes on and on.

No industry will be spared. Industries that aren't facing disruption now soon will be. Many experts believe that education and finance will be next with more to follow. Traditional companies, no matter their business, must be ready to face disruption.

Disruption is not a "set it and forget it" process, either. It evolves over time as industries continue to change due to ever-changing technology. Traditional companies must be forward-thinking. They must evolve. Data is their opportunity.

The answer is not to remain entrenched in the past, but to be ready to abandon old business models and strategies for those more suitable to the Digital Age. They must adopt digital strategies that safeguard not only their current position, but also any future success. Data is the ticket for the traditional company to not only enter, but also potentially thrive in the Digital Age. Remember, traditional companies have a lot more high-value data within their enterprises. This is an untapped goldmine.

Adapt or Perish

There is no opting out of digital transformation. Successful companies carve out new strategic options for themselves; the rest *fail*. There is no middle ground here.

For all of the opportunity that digitization brings, it also harbors peril for those that fail to adapt. This poses a huge threat to existing competitive positions. External upheavals change the playing field so profoundly that business as usual is no longer an option. I do know of traditional organizations that are "waiting" for business as usual.

Anyone in a position of corporate responsibility—be it in a supervisory or top-management capacity—should be asking himself whether or not his company is prepared to face digital disruption.

The game is changing. It's more competitive. In the face of disruption, the odds have gotten longer for traditional companies.

There are two main reasons that companies today fail:

- Management fails to make the right decisions at the right time, or;
- External upheavals change the playing field so profoundly that business as usual is simply no longer an option.
- This can be a chicken-or-the-egg problem. All too often, the first case is a function of the second: company leadership fails to ensure that the right data ends up in the hands of the right people in a timely manner.

The reverse can be true as well; relevant external data is often not captured or tracked well enough to support management decision making.

In short, management needs data in order to make good decisions and there must be a data strategy in place to ensure that this happens. In today's rapidly changing world, there is no longer the luxury of slow or inexact decision making. Data must be well organized and in the hands of the right people so that it supports managerial and executive decisions.

Business outcomes are a function of decision making. Good, prompt decisions result in good outcomes; bad decisions result in poor outcomes and business failure.

In order to maximize your company's chances of success, the right data must be in the hands of the right people so that executives have a view of the whole picture when they need it; **in today's world, that means *in real time.***

But all too often, traditional companies are operating behind the curve. Their data isn't organized for immediate use. They may be missing relevant data without even knowing it.

Companies need to set processes and organize data in order to be ready for the Digital Age. For example, consider companies that don't track consumer online behavior and social media platforms. This results in missed opportunities to better understand customer behavior and drive. It is a case of external data not utilized within the business process to add value.

The end result is missed insights and poor executive decisions due to incomplete information, and, ultimately, company failure.

Data is the answer for traditional companies looking to position themselves for success in the Digital Age. It is their best tool to compete against the Digital Natives. Why? Because it is what the Digital Natives are using.

You bring a gun to a gunfight and knives to a knife fight. Well, this is a data fight. Traditional companies must leverage the same tools as the Digital Natives.

Traditional companies don't necessarily have to look like digital companies, but they do need to have a data strategy and a digital strategy in the age of big data. They have to pivot into a digital business model.

This is a true pivot; it requires not just a data strategy, but new business processes that incorporate data. Remember: internal data reflects the organization's business process, which in turn reflects the business model. The business model itself is a consequence of the business strategy.

In the Digital Age, that strategy and model must be fully integrated with data and digital technologies. The right data strategies will capture the right and relevant data, organize it properly, enrich and integrate that data, and ultimately use it for consumption.

The right data strategy will treat data as an asset and a capability and be seamlessly and logically integrated into the business model. This is how the Digital Natives do things and there is no way that traditional companies can continue to compete without following suit.

Traditional Banks in the Digital Age: A Case Study

Let's now look at the problems faced by traditional banks operating in the Digital Age.

I do a lot of consulting in the banking industry. One of my clients, a traditional Swiss bank, held close to eighty petabytes of data. This was a wealth of potential value, but the data was not well organized.

They had no data strategy. The business model was a traditional one with traditional processes that failed to organize and use the data. Everything was, for the most part, logged on paper or on clunky mainframes. This data was trapped and not easily or efficiently consumable. The bank was using business processes that failed to value and capitalize on its data assets.

This is not an isolated case. Traditional businesses have weak business processes that aren't suitable for the Digital Age. This is reflected in their

Compare the 'digital performance' of PayPal, a digital native, with traditional swiss banks

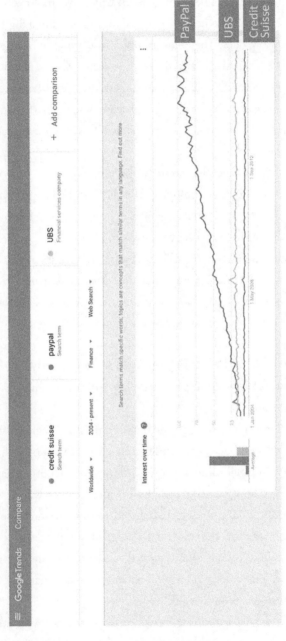

Source: https://www.google.com/trends/

Date: Oct 2016

data practices, which are typically haphazard—at best. The end result is low-quality insights and information. In turn, this leads to subpar executive decision making. In the fast-paced Digital Age, subpar won't get you very far.

In order to survive, traditional banks (and all traditional companies) must make data centric to *all* business processes and strategies. It matters at every level. Data must be leveraged on every front. Sound digital strategies must be employed in every department.

Consider, for example, digital presence. This is paramount to success in today's age. Smart companies, be they Digital Natives or adaptive legacy companies, are making proper investments.

Google Trends can be used to see the resounding success that PayPal has had in capturing digital presence as compared to Credit Suisse and UBS two traditional banks:

From this chart, it may appear as if there is no hope. But there is. It is true that traditional banks cannot stop Digital Natives from capturing market share, but they can compete in their own industries.

The traditional companies that are staying relevant are investing in digital strategies. The Google Trends chart, below, compares the 'digital presence', i.e., as 'Interest over time' of a few selected traditional banks with other banks that have invested in data and digital strategies.

Banks that are performing poorly or below average aren't making data strategy central to their business strategy. They don't understand the value of data, and they are not leveraging it properly.

They haven't realized that data is an important measure of valuation in the Digital Age, as proven by the Digital Natives, who leverage large user bases to mine data.

This can be seen at every level of the company. Just trying to determine the size of a traditional bank's customer base is difficult when processes aren't set up to capture and consume that data. People

Proof of disruption and how data can help

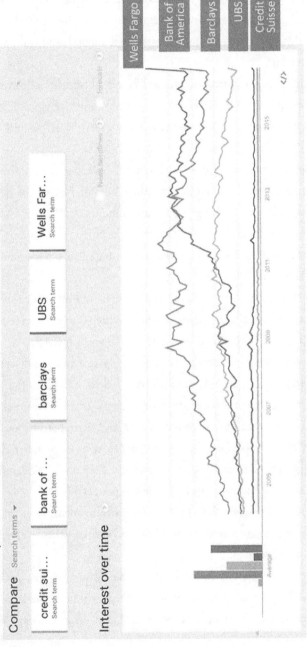

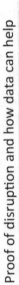

Source: https://www.google.com/trends/
Date: July 2016

responsible for management information will tell you that it depends on what you consider a "customer"—a sarcastic response.

Product Managers will tell you they know how many customers use the product they are in charge of, but that they don't know or care how many customers use other products.

Finance will simply tell you they don't care because it isn't their purview. Unfortunately, this is true; it isn't the purview of *anyone* because there aren't business processes in place to ensure that it is.

These are large institutions with a lot of institutional inertia. In order to get a handle on their business strategy, they need to get back to the basics and manage data with some concrete, fundamental measures[**]:

- Total number of customers
  — individuals
- Total number of customers
  — nonindividuals
- Average revenue per customer
  — both individuals and nonindividuals
- Profit/loss per customer
- Total number of products or services
- Total number of products or services per customer
- Total number of customer segments
- Total number of sales channels
- Profitability of sales channels

These might seem like commonplace controls, but implementing them is not always easy for a large institution that employs tens of thousands of people globally.

[**]   *This list is not exhaustive.*

Traditional companies may struggle to implement controls consistently and systematically. It can be done, but it takes work and strategy.

Unfortunately, it is not enough for traditional companies to merely understand their own industries and how to better use data. They must also understand the ways in which their industry is being disrupted by the Digital Natives. This isn't about "fixing" traditional companies. It is about adapting them to changing circumstances.

This is an active process. Traditional companies are not Digital Natives. They don't have the luxury of business models that are organic to the Digital Age, as the Digital Natives do. They must develop business processes that are visible to the customer base and provide real value, just as the Digital Natives do, but they must do so by adapting their legacy company to the new world.

In this way, traditional companies can compete with their digital disruptors. And here is how:

Step 1: Understand their current business model and adapt it to the digital world.

Step 2: Get a handle on their existing data and create a data strategy for the digital world.

Step 3: Execute on that strategy and consistently measure and monitor progress.

The takeaway here is that, at every step of the way, **data is key.**

Data is key to understanding and adapting the business model. Data gives companies a handle on their business processes. Data benefits the business strategy in real time when it is used as a capability and it can also be leveraged as an asset.

Finally, data can be used to collect information on how the business model is working, as well as to help companies pivot and adjust correctly for maximum value and growth.

Data and digital strategies must be integrated into the business model at every level. This requires a willingness to make full pivot and change strategies, processes, and the very way a company operates. It may necessitate entirely new goals. Your digital business model may, in the end, bear less resemblance to the old, traditional one than you ever could have imagined.

Don't fear this radical change; embrace it.

Companies can pivot and change their business models. There are even tools for doing so, such as the Business Model Canvas developed by Alexander Osterwalder in 2008, and since refined and added onto by others. This tool can help take complex business models and break them down into their constituent pieces in a simple template form. Such a perspective allows you to see a company's value proposition, partners, expenditures, allocations, and many other key components of the business model. (Later chapters of this book will examine the business model of data in an enterprise.)

The digital options available to businesses are growing exponentially with no sign of letting up. This affords opportunity to early adopters, like the Digital Natives, but spells peril for traditional companies that fail or struggle to keep pace.

Don't let your company fall prey to disruption. Accept it as the new lay of the land, pivot, and adapt. Let data guide the way. "May the Force be with you!"

CHAPTER 7

WHAT THE LIFE CYCLE OF DATA SAYS ABOUT YOUR ENTERPRISE

"Any enterprise CEO really ought to be able to ask a question that involves connecting data across the organization, be able to run a company effectively, and especially to be able to respond to unexpected events. Most organizations are missing this ability to connect all the data together."
—**Tim Berners-Lee**, Inventor of the World Wide Web

D
ata is valuable because it can tell us stories in the form of information and insights. You want to extract the maximum value from data. In other words, you want to get the *whole* story. No one starts a novel on page ten, skims over the middle chapters, and sets the book down just before the climax. Readers have to follow the story from beginning to end.

The same is true of data, which has a well-defined life cycle. In order to extract its maximum value, data must be appropriately managed and utilized at every stage of the life cycle.

The life cycle of data has been best described by IBM as a seven-step process:

1. Create
2. Use
3. Share
4. Update
5. Archive
6. Store/Retain
7. Dispose

This life cycle has not changed over time. Today, as in the past, data goes through this same process from life (creation) to death (disposal). Between these two points, newly inbound data is used, shared, updated, archived, and stored. It is then finally disposed of once it is no longer of use nor is relevant to the business.

All this happens within the context of business processes. For example, a hotel checks in guests as part of a business process, which leaves a data trail behind. Within this life cycle, that data will be created when the guest checks in, then used, shared with relevant process stakeholders, updated, archived and stored somewhere, and ultimately disposed of when it is no longer relevant and useful.

At every step of the way, this data has the potential to create value and be used in other business processes. Companies must understand how the life cycle of data behaves in their own business context in order to make optimal business decisions at every stage of the data life cycle. For example, the insights on guest check-ins could be shared with nearby entertainment establishments, airlines, or subsidiary companies (of course, after considering customer preferences, legals, etc.). Failure to properly utilize the data anywhere in the data life cycle results in lost opportunity and uncaptured value.

This often happens when data is either disposed of too early or, more commonly, archived as "dead data" that is never used. In large financial institutions, this data is typically stored for compliance reasons and its value is never given a second thought. For example, the records and information management department at most traditional banks may store millions of documents per year in a document-management system. These documents typically enter a black hole. The data is not used for any kind of analytics whatsoever and simply takes up space, wasting resources without providing any of its potential value.

Conversely, data is often mishandled in the creation stage, resulting in much inbound data being missed. Traditional companies tend to mismanage data at every step of the way. They don't understand that data is a reflection of the business processes and that the data life cycle must be managed within the specific context of the business. Right now, data isn't getting its due at most traditional companies. They typically only consider the data life cycle when rolling out new infrastructure or programs. Consultants are hired whenever a new system or program is rolled out. These systems are typically deployed and summarily forgotten. The data life cycle is rarely actually considered in day-to-day operations.

This is a mistake. By definition, data has value throughout its life cycle. Value should be derived as such. Emerging technologies are able to make use of data in new ways that extend its usefulness and augment its value. Companies need to unlock their data by casting aside the store-it-and-forget-it mentality and, instead, use data *within* the business processes over the entirety of its life cycle.

Data that is not managed over the entirety of its life cycle results in unrealized value. This happens every day in corporates at almost every company. To address this failure, traditional companies need to structure and organize data differently. Most enterprises store data in a fragmented manner. In large organizations, data is kept in "silos" that are typically scattered across systems and even physical geographies. This fragmented approach is a default one and doesn't have an eye toward structuring data to create value for the business. It isn't structured to appropriately handle data across its entire life cycle.

Right now, traditional companies are trying to solve their data problems by throwing more money at the latest technologies. This is like placing more emphasis on the binding and typesetting of a book than the actual words. What matters is the story—the information, insights, and, ultimately, solutions that data provides when it becomes usable information. Companies need to understand the whole story by understanding the life cycle, as well as the business context, of their data. Then, and only then, can they utilize the *right data* at the *right time* to deliver true *enterprise value*.

Tools and technology do matter. You want to use the right tools for the job; however, companies cannot possibly know what tool to use before they know or even understand the business process they are seeking to improve. Companies need to understand the life cycle of their business data before they can manage it appropriately with the right tools and technologies.

Managing the Data Life Cycle in the Digital Age

The data deluge is upon us. Total data volumes are going up exponentially across the business world. More queries are executed now than ever before. Infrastructure and IT spending are expanding in an effort to keep up. Typical data warehouses, of which some large companies may have more than one, are working with data volumes measured in petabytes or larger units. This volume of data slows down systems, increases response times on queries, and ultimately undermines business operations and efficiency.

Everything gets harder: Data management gets harder. Testing gets harder. Security is no longer as reliable. This poses not only operational and legal risks, but also reputational risks in the event of a major breach. In their 2012 Global Reputational Risk and IT Study, IBM noted that data theft/cybercrime is now the biggest threat to a company's reputation.

Handling all of this is neither easy nor cheap. Infrastructure and operational costs are through the roof. Companies need ever-greater storage capacity, which means more hardware and more technicians. For many organizations, spending on infrastructure and operations now consumes the majority of the IT budget.

Better data management is the only answer to these rising challenges and costs. In the face of the data deluge, companies must manage data effectively across its entire life cycle in order to protect performance and margins while simultaneously minimizing risks. Of course, this is easier said than done. Managing the data life cycle of data is complex today— but it can be accomplished. However, it will require shifts in the way data is structured and organized.

Historically, traditional companies have done a poor job of structuring and organizing their data. Far from a priority, data management is an afterthought, if companies consider it at all. Typically, they don't. Many traditional companies don't even have a comprehensive data strategy. Even if they do, they rarely structure data in line with that strategy across the data life cycle.

This has serious consequences. Understanding the life cycle of data is critical to making the right business decisions. I experienced this firsthand in the summer of 2006. I was leading a request for proposal (RFP) development project for a large mobile company operating in Egypt and Algeria. To be blunt, they were not managing their data well. (My tip-off should have been that they were managing the mobile network configuration on spreadsheets rather than in a relational database.) They wanted me to create an RFP for a data warehouse where global vendors could participate in a bidding process.

After reviewing their systems, we realized that they didn't actually need a data warehouse. Their IT department was already running a data warehouse that should fulfill this role, but the network-engineering department was dismissing it as an irrelevant "IT achievement." What the company actually needed was an operational data store (ODS) to support the network operations, not a data warehouse.

The executives calling the shots didn't realize that an operational data store (ODS) is what they actually wanted in order to make operational decisions. Their need was not to create a historic data store. They didn't understand the difference between the ODS and a data warehouse because they didn't understand the life cycle of their data. They were seeking the wrong tool for the wrong job.

These kinds of foundational misunderstandings are not rare among traditional companies. I just worked with a large financial institution suffering from a similar confusion. I see this all the time, in fact. Traditional companies make bad business decisions around data because they don't understand their own needs.

However, if companies would come to understand the life cycle of their data in the context of their business processes, these needs would be clear and the best solutions would be made available. They would understand their needs and identify a solution for each step in the data value chain.

This would all be clear because the steps would be tied to actual business processes. For example, in the case of my client operating in Egypt and Algeria, they would have by necessity known the differences in utility of an operational data store versus a data warehouse versus a data mart. Each of those tools is a functional solution to a different link in the data value chain, each one tied to actual business processes.

Extend this same principle to the choices your enterprise would have to make in relation to a data lake. Where does the data lake sit in relation to the life cycle of data?

The cost of failure here is high. Companies that fail to manage the life cycle of data appropriately suffer from organizational inefficiencies and depleting value. They miss out on opportunities and efficiencies. They are saddled with suboptimal legacy business processes. Their insights are flawed or incomplete. In short, they are dying enterprises.

On the other hand, organizations that appropriately manage the life cycle of their data are creating enterprise value in the process. They organize their data more efficiently, produce superior insights, and enjoy greater resiliency. They are more competitive and successful. They are faster growing. They are in control of their present and future. They use the right data at the right time to make the right decisions. They have a better chance of being in control of their destiny.

Managing the Data Value Chain

In order to structure and organize data in a logical manner across the data life cycle, companies must understand the data value chain. This is simply a way to structure data management in a way that accounts for data across its entire life cycle. The data value chain comprises two halves: the inbound processing pattern and the outbound processing pattern.

The inbound processing pattern, the data supply chain, takes data from acquisition through to analytics and consumption. Data comes in from many varied sources, is winnowed down for relevancy, enriched, analyzed, and ultimately consumed in order to provide valuable information. In short, it is the processing pattern by which inbound data is transformed into information.

The data supply chain is a six-step process:

1. Identify and Acquire
2. Catalogue and Cleanse
3. Advance Extract, Transform, and Load (ETL)
4. Prepare for Consumers
5. Management Information and Reporting
6. Advanced Visualization, Predictive and Prescriptive Analytics

This process is best thought of as a "Fibonacci spiral" funnel that channels inbound data from acquisition through to analytics. Upon acquisition, data is assigned measurable values on an index that gauges its relative importance. From there, valuable data is moved toward consumption. The graph, below, maps out this process.

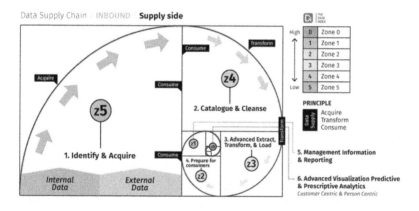

At the center of the spiral is the consumption phase. As the name suggests, this is where data is made ready for consumption. This phase is where data achieves its greatest value by being made into actual information that offers valuable insights. Companies should be focusing the majority of their IT dollars and other resources here.

To get the most out of the consumption phase, invest in the types of consumption that are best at transforming data into usable information, such as predictive and prescriptive analytics and visualizations. These tools are the best at providing high-value insights and information because they make data easier to comprehend. They tell stories—stories that are easier to understand. They create emotion. They drive action. Actions dictate outcomes.

This is key: companies must pursue person-centric analytics. Ultimately, it is people who create value through their interactions, whether they are customers, employees, partners, or other stakeholders. Person-centric analytics, therefore, provide the greatest returns. Invest accordingly.

While consumption is where the majority of IT dollars should go, the entire data value chain is important. Data doesn't become information automatically. Data must be carefully shepherded toward consumption. This is where careful organization and structuring of data becomes important. Companies must ensure they have a platform or framework that handles inbound data appropriately through its entire life, from acquisition to consumption. They must develop infrastructure, software, and systems that approach data from a life cycle perspective—that is, one that carries data from acquisition through to transformation and then to consumption.

Essentially, companies must create an economically optimized infrastructure that allows them to *acquire, transform,* and *consume* data. Broken down, the data supply chain is really just the process by which inbound data moves through these processes. Managed well at every stage, this can allow for maximum value to be extracted. We have already discussed strategies for each phase in previous chapters. For data acquisition, you want to "Cut the CRAP." For data transformation, you want to "Stay with SCRUD." (Refer back to Chapter 3 for details.) And when it comes to data consumption you want to "Set Your Anchor VARPP" by investing in high-value, person-centric analytics and consumption.

Done correctly in this way, the data supply chain can be mapped against the data life cycle. This can be seen in the below chart.

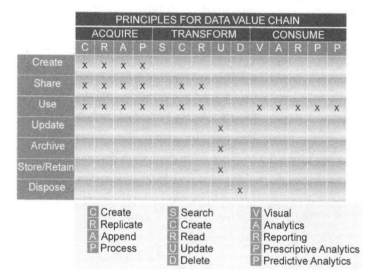

	PRINCIPLES FOR DATA VALUE CHAIN												
	ACQUIRE				TRANSFORM					CONSUME			
	C	R	A	P	S	C	R	U	D	V	A	R	P	P
Create	x	x	x	x										
Share	x	x	x	x	x	x								
Use	x	x	x	x	x	x	x			x	x	x	x	x
Update								x						
Archive								x						
Store/Retain								x						
Dispose									x					

C Create	S Search	V Visual
R Replicate	C Create	A Analytics
A Append	R Read	R Reporting
P Process	U Update	P Prescriptive Analytics
	D Delete	P Predictive Analytics

The Information Supply Chain

The data value chain doesn't end at consumption. Once inbound data is consumed and turned into information, this information has to go through an outbound process. The information supply chain is a seven-step process:

- Discovery: Take in *relevant* information from data consumption.
- Ingest: Store and structure the information *once* only.
- Process: Prepare information for *quick* use.
- Persist: *Secure* the information in a safe and compliant manner.
- Integrate: Recombine information *for greater value.*
- Analyze: Look for *insights and answers.*
- Expose: Share the information with relevant parties *to reflect business vision.*

Like the data supply chain, the information supply chain should also be mapped against the data life cycle. Each phase of the outbound process is guided by a set of simple principles.

	PRINCIPLES FOR INFORMATION LIFE CYCLE						
	Relevant	Once	Fast	Securely & Legally	For Value	To Answer	To Reflect Vision
	INFORMATION LIFE CYCLE						
	Discover	Ingest	Process	Persists	Integrate	Analyze	Expose
Create	X				X	X	
Share	X	X	X		X	X	X
Use	X	X	X		X	X	X
Update	X	X	X		X	X	
Archive	X		X	X			
Store/Retain	X	X	X	X	X		
Dispose	X						

In the outbound process, information moves from discover to expose, in which it produces its own new internal and external data. The outbound process also exists as a funnel—this time, spiraling outward as the information is reintegrated and expands into more consumable and insightful data.

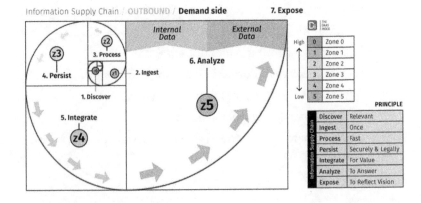

The data supply chain and the information supply chain are two sides of a larger process: the data value chain. The first is a funnel that "crunches" inbound data down into information by preparing and transforming if for consumption. The second is an outbound process that funnels information outward from discovery to exposure, disseminating internally and externally in the form of new data.

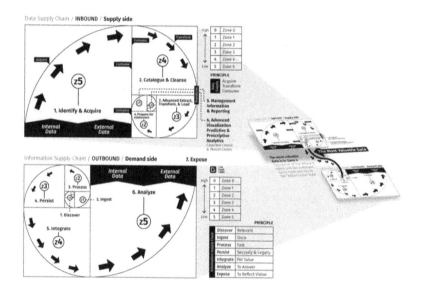

The most important takeaway here is that the narrow area where the two spirals meet at the center of the data value chain is where data becomes information. This is the beginning of the consumption phase, where data is in its most valuable raw form, and the ingestion phase is where information gains its maximum potential. This is where the majority of IT investments should be made, particularly on consumption.

However, this entire model is predicated on carefully shepherding inbound data from acquisition to consumption, and then the resulting outbound information out to exposure as new data. To get the most out of data, and consequentially, the most out of the consumption phase itself, data must be managed carefully across the entire data life cycle and value chain, from beginning to end.

CHAPTER 8

GOING DIGITAL GLOBALLY: THE RIGHT WAY TO DO IT

"Digital is the main reason just over half of the companies on the Fortune 500 have disappeared since the year 2000."
—**Pierre Nanterme**, Chairman and CEO of Accenture

There is a chasm dividing the way that traditional companies approach data from the way the Digital Natives do. This is because the Digital Natives, being newer, developed data strategies that are most conducive to the Digital Age. Traditional companies are saddled with legacy data strategies—if they have one at all. To compete in the Digital Age, traditional companies must approach data strategy more like the Digital Natives do.

The Digital Natives have developed data strategies that balance regulatory compliances and growth adequately, achieving greater enterprise value and business process automation.

Automation is critical in business today. In the past, most business processes were isolated. This was fine in the non-digital world, but the Digital Age has ushered in an era of total business and consumer globalism. In this context, business processes need to be automated so that they will operate seamlessly across the entire globe. Amazon.com is a good example of this; their store works the same for consumers regardless of where they live. This is not the case, for example, with Swiss businesses in Switzerland, where I live. Using a Swiss bank here is very different from using a bank in London, whereas Amazon.com offers services here that, while tailored to the local community, are integrated seamlessly into the Amazon.com model. The experience for the consumer, regardless of location, is the same.

The advantages of maximizing enterprise value and increasing compliance efficiency are obvious. However, striking the right balance is critical.

Thus, getting the balancing act right will move traditional companies closer to the Digital Natives and their higher valuations. This is a journey

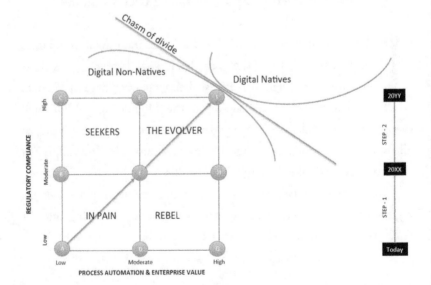

that traditional companies must make. Right now, they face great pain because of their outdated data strategies. This journey is depicted in the chart on the previous page.

Currently, most traditional companies are in the bottom left corner of the chart, opposite the Digital Natives. Traditional companies must approach the "chasm of divide" by operating more like the Digital Natives. Traditional companies need to focus on at least two things to make this journey. First, they must use data-management practices to meet minimum regulatory compliance needs (y-axis). An example of this is the BCBS 239 compliance for banks or the Solvency II Directive for insurance companies. Second, they must improve business process automation and enterprise value (x-axis) for higher growth.

The most effective and efficient way for companies to make this journey is in a straight line, moving progressively from the bottom left to the top right, i.e., striking the right balance. This will move companies away from their current "pain," as they become digital "evolvers" that have managed to step into the Digital Age. This is the optimal path.

Unfortunately, it is not always the one that companies make when attempting to go digital. All too often, they move from Point A on the grid to Point B, and then to Point C. This often happens because traditional companies base their digital strategies primarily around compliance matters—they look mostly at the data they are required to have on hand to meet compliance and regulatory needs. These companies become "seekers"; they are looking to go digital, but are lost because they aren't actually increasing efficiency or enterprise value.

Other companies go digital by moving from Point A to Point D, and then to Point G. These companies have invested in business process automation and are building enterprise value, as they should, but by ignoring compliance, they may be branded as "rebels." They are likely to see monetary success, but may run afoul of regulatory bodies.

Both seeker and rebel companies may eventually evolve and approach the "evolved" status of companies that have become more like the Digital Natives by updating their data strategies for the Digital Age. However, when making the smart choice to go digital, traditional companies should take the most direct path toward the chasm that now divides them from the Digital Natives.

The chasm need only be approached, not necessarily traversed. Traditional companies are not the Digital Natives. They typically run different kinds of businesses. They carved out their niche before the territory that the Digital Natives filled, even existed. The two are not *necessarily* in direct competition (though sometimes they are). Hotels and insurance companies don't need to rush out and build the next big online marketplace or social media application. They simply need to embrace the Digital Age by going digital and doing what they do best— the only difference being, doing it digitally.

What We Mean by "Going Digital"

What does it mean to go digital? Traditional companies cannot undertake this journey without first defining it.

According to McKinsey & Company, a large global consulting firm helping global companies in the Digital Age, digital shouldn't be thought of as a *thing* so much as a *way of doing things*. They described going digital as meaning three things:

- being open to new ways of doing business in order to build value at new frontiers;
- creating value in core businesses through automation, innovation, and interactivity;
- and building the right foundational capabilities.

Creating value at new frontiers comes down to looking for undiscovered value—particularly value that emerging technologies have unlocked. This becomes exceedingly important in a global environment in which global companies have access to new markets.

Geography is purely a matter of choice in the Digital Age. The personal identity of your customers is more important than their nationality or locale. Look for new customer prospects unlocked by technology as well as new ways to engage current customers. At the end of the day, business is just putting your product or services in the hands of those who want it. Develop a customer-centric business model.

Ask yourself, *Where can I find new customers? How can I serve them? How will they react and respond to my company?* In essence, *Who are they and what do they want?* Once you know this, you can start identifying and developing new business processes to serve these new prospects, regardless of their nationality. Do that, and new prospects will become new customers.

In addition to building value through new customers, traditional companies stand to gain new value by using automation, innovation, and interactivity to produce more value in their long-standing core business areas. New digital tools and strategies can be applied to the core business in order to increase efficiency and produce greater gains. In other words, use emerging technologies not just to find new customers, but also to better serve your current customers. Technology can help companies master and manage their core business processes.

In short, companies need to use digital technologies to shore up existing business processes while also developing new ones that weren't possible without newer technologies. The chart below illustrates different ways in which companies can create value by addressing both supply and demand for their products/services by factoring data into the equation.

We have partially addressed these first two points in previous chapters. However, we have not yet addressed McKinsey & Company's

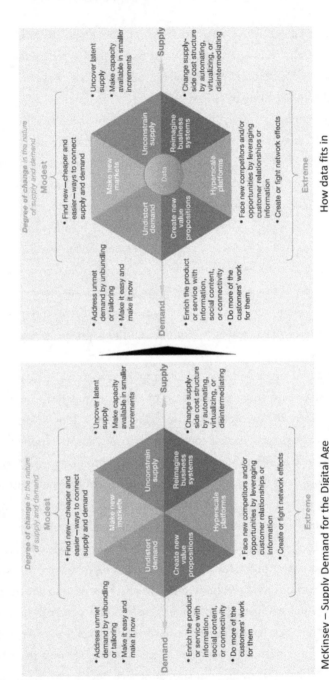

McKinsey – Supply Demand for the Digital Age

third key tenet of going digital: building the right foundational capabilities for the Digital Age.

Building Foundational Capabilities

While much of going digital involves strategy, there is an element of nuts-and-bolts data architecture involved in taking a company digital. Traditional companies must build data systems architecture that is appropriate to the Digital Age.

To that end, system and data architectures built today must be:

- Business-model resilient and able to actually serve the business model
- Customer-centric, person-centric, and data-centric
- Collaborative and outcome-oriented
- Secure and compliant to regulations

In the previous chapter, we looked at how to map the data life cycle against the business model. The data life cycle starts with the creation of data, which is then processed, transformed, and fed to data repositories known as operational data stores (ODS). Bill Inmon, a groundbreaking computer scientist widely recognized as the "Father of Data Warehousing," described the ODS as "an integrated, subject-oriented, volatile (including update), current-valued structure designed to serve operational users as they do high-performance integrated processing." The ODS supports operational decision making.

The ODS is not new and will be familiar to IT professionals. Since the 1990s, and up until now, the ODS, along with the data warehouse, has been an integral component of the data and information architecture landscape for all companies. But, has this information architecture actually provided exceptional outcomes to most enterprises? In some cases, it has certainly provided satisfactory, or even good, outcomes—but exceptional or delightful outcomes are probably a stretch.

Data warehousing has come a long way as the field of information technology has progressed. Pioneers of information management, such as Bill Inmon and Claudia Imhoff, have paved the way for business organizations to convert their raw data into information of actual value—*substantial* value. Many constraints and challenges have been overcome. Data warehouses today are more efficient and effective.

However, information technologists still have much work to do. Business organizations and departments serviced by IT functions are unlikely to describe IT departments as "delightful" partners. For that to happen, Information Technologists need to think more like business

CLASS-N
FOR THE AGE OF BIG DATA

	DATA STRATEGY	BUILD COMPLEXITY	NOTES
CLASS 0	Wholesale Table Replication	Easy to Build	• No data integration • Data ages quickly • For small volumes only* • ODS data not fit DWH
CLASS I	Transaction Replication	Slightly Complicated to Build	• No integration • A collection of transactions • ODS data not fit for DWH
CLASS II	Integration of Transactions	Complex to Build	• Complexity of integration • Slower movement into ODS • ODS data fit for DWH
CLASS III	Aggregated Analyzed Data Warehouse Data	Reasonably Easy to build	• Very flexible • Way to get analytic data to the customer at the point of interaction
CLASS IV	Integrated Transactions, Aggregated Data Warehouse Data	Complex to Build	• Requires planning • Complex • Greatest payoff • Lengthy time build

Different Classes of ODS based on how fast the data is loaded into the ODS people. They need to ask themselves how technology and data, including their company's application ecosystem, can be used to create business value. **They need to provide a customer-centric, outcome-oriented data architecture that actually serves the business model.**

Let's look at the ODS as an example. Inmon originally described the various classes of operational data stores, each with its own advantages and drawbacks.

What many companies don't realize is that data can now be fed into a single catchall repository known as a Class-N ODS that combines all of the four classes described by Inmon. This is depicted in the following chart.

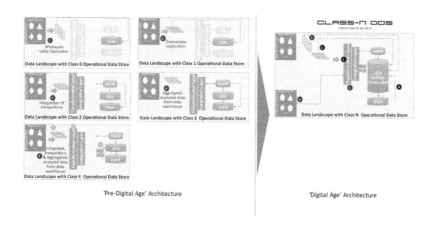

'Pre-Digital Age' Architecture   'Digital Age' Architecture

Some vendors refer to this catchall repository as the data lake due to its vast size and monolithic nature. However, this metaphor might give the false impression that the Class-N ODS is disorganized. This couldn't be further from the truth. This lake of data is all relevant to the business model. All business processes are aligned with the business model. All technologies collide harmoniously here. Legacy technologies meet emerging technologies gracefully. The Class-N ODS is where, in terms of data management and data engineering, everything comes together in one place. It is a one-size-fits-all data depository for all enterprises. The figure below depicts the Class-N ODS data architecture layout.

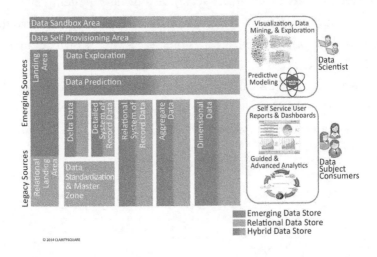

The Class-N ODS is just one example of a foundational capability that meets the four goals of systems and data architecture for the Digital Age. The same standards apply to all systems. Furthermore, these systems must be measured quantitatively to ensure they are providing true service to the greater business. There is a system for doing just this, the Data as an Asset (DAAS) Index, which we will discuss in a subsequent chapter.

Data Strategy for the Digital Enterprise

When preparing to go digital, incumbent companies must think carefully about the digital strategies that are truly available to them. Most traditional companies are not massively valued Digital Natives. Companies that can operate as pure-play disrupters at a global scale—companies such as Spotify and Uber—are few in number. Even rarer are companies that operate as "ecosystem shapers" that set de facto standards and gain command of the universal control points in their market by hyper-scaling digital platforms. Operating as a disruptor is simply not possible for most traditional companies.

Generally speaking, 95 to 99 percent of incumbent companies must choose a different path. Companies do not have to operate as disruptors in order to wholeheartedly commit themselves to a clear digital strategy that will create value at new frontiers, build value at their core business, and build out foundational capabilities to support these goals.

Companies must avoid only going digital at the margins of their established businesses. Companies that do this tend to append a "digital element" to their business, but leave the core business essentially unchanged. The digital strategy is seen as secondary and is not fully integrated into the business model. Success depends on investing in digital capabilities that are well aligned with the overall digital strategy and relevant to the business model—**and being able to do so at scale.**

The right capabilities can help companies keep pace with their customers as digitization changes consumer behavior. However, while technical capabilities (e.g., big-data analytics, digital content management, and search engine optimization) are crucial to success in the Digital Age, a strong and adaptive culture is more important. Remember: **going digital is not about things; it's about how you do things.** Companies need to align their technology strategy, data strategy, organizational structures, talent development, capital allocations, funding mechanisms, and key operations with the new digital strategy.

Developing and Implementing a Global Digital Strategy

Digital strategies are multifaceted and complex. Developing and implementing the *right* one is neither straightforward nor easy. Rarely will two companies have the same optimal digital strategy.

However, while digital strategies will vary across companies, there is a systematic and uniform method for developing and implementing the right global digital strategy. This is an eight-step process:

1. Review your business model.
2. Identify key business processes.
3. Document the current application landscape supporting the key business processes.
4. Use your business processes and efficiency needs to create an optimized application landscape that addresses those needs.
5. Create a new technology strategy and data strategy, or refine current ones, in order to deliver the optimal application landscape.
6. Revisit resource allocation—both methods and processes.
7. Manage resources and progress toward digital goals in a systematic and controlled manner by implementing a sound measurement system (e.g., the DAAS Index).
8. Maintain optimal digital strategy by engaging in continuous improvement via ongoing measurement, monitoring, and controls.

This is a systematic procedure for implementing a global digital strategy for any and all enterprises. Start by reviewing the business model and identifying key business processes that you want to execute at a global scale. Generally speaking, these are processes that create actual monetary value.

Document the current application landscape that supports these key business processes. These are all of the systems and applications that carry out and track business processes. Then look at your key business processes and efficiency and other business needs, and find the optimal application landscape for delivering on those needs. Here, you are mapping the business processes against your application landscape, looking for areas of improvement.

Armed with an outline of your current application landscape and a blueprint for your optimal application landscape, you can now develop a data strategy and digital strategy that will move you from the former to the latter. By following this process, you will be able to develop a data strategy that addresses your actual business needs by providing a road map to get you from where you are now to where you want to be. This strategy will highlight specific areas of improvement that address actual problems with your application landscape.

From here, companies should revisit resource allocation in order to execute on the new digital strategy. All too often, resource allocation is based on a few past projects or programs that have long since been commissioned and forgotten—yet their legacy outlives them. This is a default and suboptimal approach to IT spending. Budgets should be based on current needs, not past needs. Now that you have a digital strategy, you can be deliberate in your IT spending. You now know your IT needs and you can budget accordingly. Revisit your IT budget and ensure that outlays are well allocated.

You cannot be sure your new digital strategy is performing better unless you actually measure its performance. Manage resources and progress toward digital goals by implementing a sound measurement system. Without a proper measuring system, the digital strategy cannot be delivered in a systematic and controlled manner. Companies must have a way to measure the effectiveness of their data systems. To this end, we have introduced just such a system: the DAAS Index, which will be discussed in detail in a later chapter. For now, just understand that the DAAS Index can be used to measure the utility of data systems so that resources can be allocated toward the most important systems.

This measurement and monitoring is an ongoing process. The digital strategy must stay relevant as the business context changes. You cannot simply roll out a global digital strategy and then forget about it. Companies can only *maintain* an optimal digital strategy by engaging in continuous improvement via ongoing measurement, monitoring, and controls. Ideally, these processes and controls will be systematic and automated.

CHAPTER 9

DATA BREACHES AND HOW TO AVOID THEM

"Social security, bank account, and credit card numbers aren't just data. In the wrong hands, they can wipe out someone's life savings, wreck their credit, and cause financial ruin."
—**Melissa Bean**, American Politician

Data breaches are marching in lockstep with the proliferation of emerging data technologies. Big data comes hand in hand with security risk. This should not be surprising. As companies have gone digital, so too have crime and fraud.

Major security breaches have become the status quo. They become increasingly common each year. In many industries, the majority of companies have been affected by data breaches. Consider health care as just one example. According to an annual study on the privacy and security of health-care data, conducted by Ponemon Institute, nearly 90 percent of health-care organizations and 60 percent of their business associates were subject to data breaches in the past two years. Nearly 80 percent of health-care organizations experienced multiple data breaches.

The cost of these breaches across an entire industry can be staggering. *Infosecurity Magazine* recently reported that data breaches are costing the industry in excess of $6 billion per year. This number continues to grow.

The cost to an individual enterprise can also be enormous and crippling. When UK-based telecom company TalkTalk Group endured a major security breach in October 2015, the company lost £15 million in trading revenue and faced exceptional costs totaling as much as £45 million. The company also lost more than one hundred thousand customers within six months due to its poor handling of the crisis.

No company is immune to data breaches. Even the most exemplary Digital Natives have been affected. In 2015, Google suffered a data breach that exposed many of its employees' names, Social Security numbers, and other sensitive information. While it is true that this was caused by the reckless behavior of a third-party benefits-management service the company employed, no company can avoid using third-party vendors. In the end, it was Google that took the hit to its reputation, not the contracted company. This reputational damage can be hard to quantify, but it is very real. For a Digital Native to suffer such a breach is embarrassing and undermines confidence in their core business of technology.

The damage is not limited to the Digital Natives of course. Major traditional companies face these breaches all of the time. Walmart recently reported a data breach at a store in Fredericksburg, Virginia, that resulted in dozens of customers having their bank accounts compromised, and, in some cases, even drained of funds. These types of events can be massive, such as the 2013 incident (not made public until 2014) in which a data breach compromised the personal information of 70 million Target customers. This resulted in real and measurable economic damage. Many of the affected parties are now probably *former* customers.

Perhaps the largest such event in history was the 2014 JPMorgan Chase data breach in which internal information associated with 83 million customer accounts was compromised. Despite the name given by the media, this breach, which was carried out by hackers, actually affected ten major financial institutions—a large swath of the industry. The attack, in which cybercriminals gained high-level system privileges on more than ninety servers, went unnoticed for two months. This was despite the $250 million JPMorgan Chase was spending annually on security. The company has since pledged to double that figure in order to prevent another breach and to mitigate the reputational damage of this one.

These are but a few recent examples of data breaches. There are many more. The problem is huge and growing. No one is safe. The Digital Natives are at risk. Traditional companies, which may place less focus on IT in general, are definitely at risk. Every industry is at risk, whether it deals primarily in digital services or not. Financial institutions are at just as high of risk, perhaps greater, than Digital Native companies. Successful companies today must have a large digital component to their business model.

These breaches do real economic damage. Data breaches expose people to identity theft and fraud. This is unacceptable, even if the enterprise is financially successful. If stakeholders are not protected, the business model is not secured adequately, regardless of how much economic value is created. Of course, much of the value created will also be destroyed or damaged by the breach. Companies are on the line for losses from fraud. There are other costs too. Fines and court settlements can run into the tens of millions or more. There are costs for reimbursements, as well as auditing and consulting services following a breach.

The reputational damage to a company can be even more devastating. Security breaches, and especially poorly handled breaches, are a big mark against companies that handle sensitive information, whether the company is known for its social media platforms or its online banking services. Although reputational damages to a brand can be hard to quantify or prove, they are no less concrete. Breaches often coincide with falling stock prices, churn, and lower revenues. Following a slew of cyber attacks on US banks, Citigroup, Bank of America, and Wells Fargo showed a 0.4 to 0.9 percent drop in their stock prices. JPMorgan Chase saw its share price fall by 1 percent after the security breach mentioned above.

It is easy to become numb to data breaches given that they occur so often and the losses in currency are so high that the numbers seem incomprehensible. But the real-world effects are not just numbers on a spreadsheet. Those affected are real people suffering real consequences. The fallout faced by customers, employees, and other stakeholders—to say nothing of the companies themselves—can be immense.

Data Security—More Than Just an IT Matter

Data breaches can erase massive value overnight, harm stakeholders, and derail companies. These risks are of board-level importance and warrant serious consideration by the highest executives of a company.

Unfortunately, these risks rarely get the attention they deserve in corporate boardrooms, especially at traditional companies. C-suite executives are *aware* of the risks; they just don't see them as worthy of boardroom attention. Historically, data security was considered an IT matter. Even today, data security typically falls on the shoulders of the IT department, and the IT department alone. Data and technology are not seen as core to most traditional businesses, so boards don't give the matter personal attention.

This is a mistake. In the Digital Age, data security is not just an IT matter. Technology and data are so central to business that they must be integrated into the business model. That is the purview of the boardroom. Security must be planned at the highest levels of an enterprise and implemented throughout the entire company. It is not just up to the IT department to prevent data breaches. General counsel, finance, and other core business functions also play a major role in mitigating security risks with appropriate compliance and audit programs.

These functions are sometimes even more important than the IT department when it comes to preventing security breaches. Data breaches are not just generic data breaches. They occur for a reason and in a particular way. Data breaches are breaches of business processes. They are breaches of the technology strategy. **They are ultimately breaches of the business strategy, thereby compromising the mission and vision.**

The board is responsible for architecting the business strategy in a way that minimizes and prevents data breaches. Data breaches reflect a failure of the enterprise's vision and mission. This has never been truer than now. The Digital Age requires successful companies to integrate data strategy into the business strategy.

As these threats become increasingly common and more complex, there has never been a greater need for companies and their boards to understand their information-security risk. In general, the Digital Natives have been much better at understanding and managing information-security risks than traditional companies. Traditional companies are often saddled with business models developed before the Digital Age.

What Options Do We Have?

Ultimately, security breaches are attacks against weaknesses in the business model or particular business processes. New technology has created new security risks. Business processes that open companies up to information-security risks must be rethought. In the Digital Age, the business processes that comprise the business model have to be well considered with an eye toward minimizing data breaches and eliminating them when possible.

There are two classic security patterns in common usage:

- Securing at the perimeter
- Securing appropriately around business processes

These two strategies are not mutually exclusive; they are normally deployed together. However, even when used in combination, they both have serious limitations that make them insufficient security models for the Digital Age.

Securing at the perimeter involves putting protections at the boundaries of the entire data ecosystem. The enterprise tries to protect the whole data ecosystem as one entity by erecting a wall and protecting the gates. Unfortunately, it is nearly impossible to perfectly encapsulate and isolate the entire data ecosystem of a large global company. It is even harder to keep such a large ecosystem protected at all points of entrance. You can liken this to trying to secure a large nation by only securing at the borders. The problem with this is that the borders are often large, and, once an intruder bypasses any walls or checkpoints, he has easy access once inside the border.

This strategy also creates serious systemic risk when used alone. A single hole can allow intruders to compromise the entire system if security relies only on securing the perimeter. Once the perimeter is breached, the intruders may have the run of the place.

Securing at the perimeter is also inefficient because it places equal importance on all data and all data systems. This makes no sense. Some data is more relevant to the business model than other data. Some data is more sensitive to breach. These kinds of data deserve and demand greater protections. Resources should not be wasted over-securing unimportant data at the expense of providing greater security for more sensitive, valuable data. Companies need ways to determine the relative importance of their different data systems (for more information on how to determine which data systems are of greater relevant importance to the business model, see Chapter 10 on the DAAS Index).

Securing appropriately around business processes is a more nuanced and thorough way of securing the data ecosystem. This strategy involves placing security controls around each and every business process in order to prevent security risks where they happen. To return to our nation-state analogy, securing around the business processes would be more similar to distributed security, military, and police forces that protect public and private places on-site.

Securing around the business process, while necessary, is a challenge. Business processes change often and rapidly. The boundaries of the processes can be difficult to isolate precisely, which can result in a security hole "between" processes. The business processes must be secured, but companies today need a strategy for knowing which processes are most important for protecting their most valuable and sensitive data.

Companies must adopt a data perspective when it comes to security. This does not mean that companies must completely abandon their previous security tactics. Perimeter security can still be useful in warding off simple attacks. Securing appropriately around the business processes must still be done, but it must be done from a data-pattern perspective.

Securing by the Spiral

In previous chapters, we mapped out the data value chain, which comprises both the data supply chain and information supply chain, using the Fibonacci spiral. The data supply chain is useful when planning security because it allows companies to implement a security zoning model based around the relative importance of particular data systems.

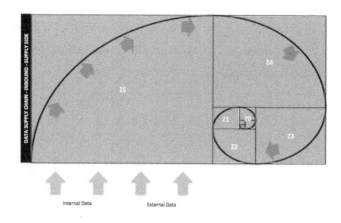

Data Security Zones – Inbound Data Supply Chain

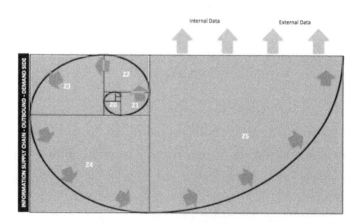

Data Security Zones – Outbound Information Supply Chain

In the above graphics, data is categorized by zone. The zone gives us the data's value and sensitivity based on its relative importance to the business model. Data gains increasing value, and also becomes increasingly sensitive to a breach, the closer it is to the center of the spiral. This relative value is demonstrated in the graphic below. The relative enterprise value of any specific data system or application can be precisely determined using a tool we call the DAAS Index, which will be discussed thoroughly in a subsequent chapter.

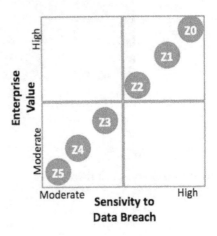

Positioning Enterprise Systems with the DAAS Index:
Enterprise Value VS Sensitivity to Data Breach

Data in Zone 0 is both the most sensitive to a breach as well as the most valuable to the enterprise. This is the **Billion Dollar Byte.** This data holds the most value and must be kept safe in order to avoid economic and reputational damage. It only makes sense to spend the most resources on securing this data.

This data is sensitive because it has now become actual insight-providing *information*. This is where enterprises extract person-centric insights, meaning that the data is now within the right and relevant context of the business model. Zone 0 contains identifying information of customers, employees, and partners, as well as relevant financial and other sensitive information. The enterprise will have collected usable data on individuals, matching their name with their financials, ordering history, identifying details, and other information. This is now sensitive contextualized information and even insights, not just isolated data. Zone 0 also contains identifying information about products and business secrets.

This data must not fall into the wrong hands—the very hands that are clawing for it right now. Companies should allocate the greatest resources to securing the business processes that surround data in Zone 0. The other zones must be secured as well, but the security-zone model allows companies to focus their security efforts *appropriately* in the right zones.

If the data value chain is already properly managed, companies do not need to make arbitrary decisions about which business processes to focus on securing. The most sensitive and valuable data can easily be identified based on which zone it falls into. The businesses processes that surround the data in each zone will already be separated because the processes for handling incoming data are different from those used to handle information in Zone 0.

For example, consider the collected data of an individual who moves from prospect to customer. Data from a prospect will be in Zone 5 when the data is first collected. By the time the prospect becomes a customer, their data will have moved to Zone 0. The processes used to handle customers are different than those used to handle prospects. The data is likely to be handled with different data systems. Securing the most valuable and sensitive data is simply a matter of placing controls around those business processes.

In this way, companies can develop a security model that is appropriate to its business model. This is **security by the spiral.** It ensures that resources are allocated to protecting data assets based on their value to the business and their sensitivity to breach. Choices don't have to be made for each business process and each data system or application; enterprises simply allocate more resources to securing business processes for data that is more valuable and sensitive to breach.

The Data-Security Checklist

When it comes to cyber security, there are several things every company, including its board, should be asking its security team right now:

- How strong is my company's current security program? How does it compare with the security programs of other companies in my industry?
- Do we know the relative importance of our systems and our data landscape adequately enough? Or are we just securing at the perimeter, which is not helpful in a digital world?
- What can we do to stop advanced threats from infiltrating our systems?
- Do we have the appropriate organizational and technological maturity to understand our business model, processes, and data landscape?
- Are we doing everything we can to protect our most valuable data?
- Do we have a holistic approach to understanding the value of our data, and the relevant processes to protect it?
- How can we adopt new technologies—such as big data analytics, mobile and cloud—without compromising our security?
- Do we have a data strategy for the digital world's realities?

CHAPTER 10

THE DAAS INDEX: "PAGE RANKING" FOR YOUR DATA

"Measure what is measurable, and make measurable what is not so."

—**Galileo Galilei**, Italian Scientist

n 1998, Larry Page and Sergey Brin published *The PageRank Citation Ranking: Bringing Order to the Web* about the work they had been doing at Stanford University. They had set out to bring order to the nascent World Wide Web by creating a new way to organize web pages for search results. Rather than ordering web pages by content, they gave each page a "PageRank" based on its relative "importance" to other web pages. They were measuring not what a page was about, but where it fit into the World Wide Web's graph structure.

This method returned higher-quality search results, and their work on PageRank laid the foundation for what would become their company,

Google, and its first flagship product: their revolutionary search engine. PageRank paved the way for all modern search engines. The Internet would never be the same again.

PageRank worked by measuring the usefulness, or value, of a web page by the number of backlinks. This is an effective measure of the demand for the web page as a specific information asset. The PageRank algorithm has been refined over the years, but Google still calculates relative importance based on a page's backlinks. Pages with greater quantity and higher quality of backlinks receive a higher PageRank value and move up the search results.

This technique establishes the demand for a particular web page, which can be thought of in this context as a digital asset. The *demand* for the piece of information in a page is the key output of the algorithm of the PageRank. This demand is a function of its inherent economic value. In other words, PageRank defined and measured demand pattern and usefulness of web pages. This made search engines more useful because, knowing which pages were more valuable, algorithms could serve up the more useful web pages. PageRank allowed Google to match supply with demand.

PageRank afforded Google a *standardized* way to serve users more relevant search results. Users were demanding relevant data and Google was now able to supply more relevant data. They could do this because PageRank identified the true value of web pages. Relevant web pages are a valuable asset to users. Google was able to achieve astronomical valuation precisely because it could monetize those assets.

The problem that Google solved via PageRank is comparable to a similar problem faced by enterprise in the age of big data. The enterprise world now deals with a vast landscape of data applications and systems. The data deluge and globalization have required companies to build out massive data infrastructures made up of hundreds or thousands of data systems. These systems are hard to manage because they are poorly organized. There is no mechanism for measuring their relative importance.

This is a big problem for companies operating in the digital world. We know that these data systems and applications are important and valuable, or no one would build them, but we don't know their relative importance. Which are most important and why? Enterprises cannot currently answer these questions because they have no easy way to measure the relative importance of their data systems in a *consistent, standardized, and governed manner.*

Introducing the DAAS Index

Recognizing this problem, my company, Claritysquare Technology, a strategy, advisory, and consulting firm based in Zürich, Switzerland, set out to create a tool that would allow companies to gauge the relative importance of their various enterprise application systems. We took inspiration from PageRank, but rather than measuring the relative importance of web pages, we were measuring the relative importance of enterprise application systems, such as data repositories, databases, data warehouses, data marts, and other data-centric systems.

These systems have value based on the data they contain, but not all data is relevant to all businesses. Data is an asset only when it is relative to the business model and processes. The more relevant a data system is within the wider context of a business, the greater its value. We sought to measure the value of enterprise systems by treating data as the asset that it is. This is how the Data as an Asset (DAAS) Index was born. We sought to quantify the value of data systems by recognizing them as assets.

The DAAS Index allows companies and executives to "measure what they treasure" when it comes to their data systems. The goal was not to rank data systems by their *independent* value, but by their *relative* value. We wanted to be able to tell companies what data systems were worth in the context of the business. Adopting the DAAS Index finally gives enterprises a consistent, standardized, and governable system for understanding the relative importance of their data systems. It is a tool that gives companies and their executives a mechanism for gauging the relative importance of data systems.

The Nine Key Parameters of the DAAS Index

The DAAS Index is a quantified measurement that assigns a scaled numerical value to individual data systems in large enterprises with complex data ecosystems. The index value is derived from a set of defined parameters that measure enterprise value in economic terms.

These nine parameters are simple in concept but extremely nuanced. Quantifying and combining them into a single index value that is both accurate and holistic is no easy task, though it can be done. Database systems are no more complex than the Internet. Google PageRank effectively organized the Internet according to user demand, and the DAAS Index is fully capable of doing the same for enterprise data ecosystems.

The DAAS Index does this by functioning as a 'data asset demand estimator'. Whereas PageRank measures the demand for a web page based on its backlinks and position within the greater web, the DAAS Index measures the demand for a system or application by measuring and quantifying its relative value to stakeholders and its relative usefulness to the rest of the enterprise. In this way, the relative importance of the application can be quantified and known, allowing supply and demand to be matched.

In other words, armed with this knowledge, companies are better positioned to make sound, informed business decisions about their IT-system investments and spending. In the case of Fortune 500 companies, these outlays easily run into the millions, and even billions. Suboptimal choices about where and how to make these investments is costly. Even

Data as an Asset (DAAS) Index

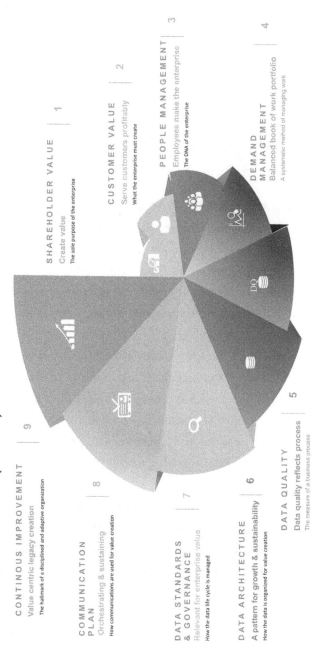

CONTINOUS IMPROVEMENT | 9
Value centric legacy creation
The hallmark of a disciplined and adaptive organization

COMMUNICATION PLAN | 8
Orchestrating & sustaining
How communications are used for value creation

DATA STANDARDS & GOVERNANCE | 7
Relevant for enterprise value
How the data life cycle is managed

DATA ARCHITECTURE | 6
A pattern for growth & sustainability
How the data is organized for value creation

DATA QUALITY | 5
Data quality reflects process
The measure of a business process

SHAREHOLDER VALUE | 1
Create value
The sole purpose of the enterprise

CUSTOMER VALUE | 2
Serve customers profitably
What the enterprise must create

PEOPLE MANAGEMENT | 3
Employees make the enterprise
The DNA of the enterprise

DEMAND MANAGEMENT | 4
Balanced book of work portfolio
A systematic method of managing work

*Patent Pending, USPTO

© Claritysquare Technology GmbH, 2015

minor inefficiencies can be extremely expensive when working with such giant outlays.

Misallocation of funds does more than waste money; it leads to value errosion when the data-centric initiatives and investments do not create value. With the DAAS Index, companies can be sure they have the right system solutions in place to meet their actual needs and deliver massive economic value, in a controlled and transparent manner.

Implement the DAAS Index in Your Organization

Because it measures the relative value of systems, the DAAS Index must be implemented carefully across the entire ecosystem in order to achieve accurate measurements. The DAAS Index provides a *relative* index value that is most meaningful and of economic value when it is used as a tool for standardization of measurement and assessment across the entire enterprise.

Claritysquare Technology has developed a nine-step process for implementing and maintaining the DAAS Index in an enterprise:

This method is a tried and proven technique for bringing order to enterprise data systems. The process starts by first establishing the scope of each enterprise application. Companies first identify all of their data systems and applications. You have to define what you are measuring before you can assign it a value.

Next, you must identify stakeholders for each system. This may be a diverse crowd of stakeholders because they will not be the same stakeholders across the entire enterprise—not for large companies. These stakeholders will have various, sometimes even competing, interests. The thing that ties them together is that they all have an *economic* interest in the enterprise's value.

Once identified, stakeholders are then interviewed and assessed based upon nine DAAS Index parameters. Companies must also

Nine Steps to Implement the DAAS Index in an Enterprise

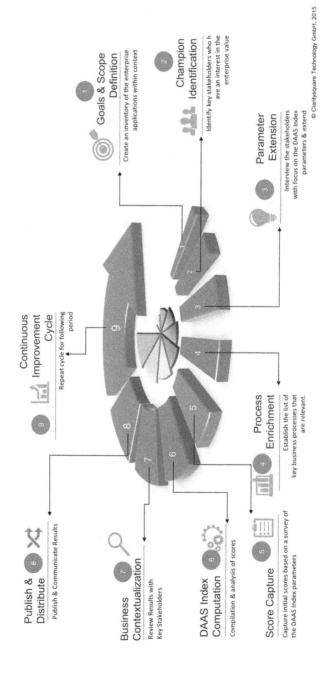

Goals & Scope Definition
Create an inventory of the enterprise applications within context

Champion Identification
Identify key stakeholders who have an interest in the enterprise value

Parameter Extension
Interview the stakeholders with focus on the DAAS Index parameters & extend

Process Enrichment
Establish the list of key business processes that are relevant.

Score Capture
Capture initial scores based on a survey of the DAAS Index parameters

DAAS Index Computation
Compilation & analysis of scores

Business Contextualization
Review Results with Key Stakeholders

Publish & Distribute
Publish & Communicate Results

Continuous Improvement Cycle
Repeat cycle for following period

© Claritysquare Technology GmbH, 2015

identify the specific business processes that are of value to the individual stakeholders, as well as the enterprise systems or applications that are tied to these processes. These are extension and enrichment processes in which companies investigate why their systems are valuable and to whom.

With this information in hand, you can derive an initial score for each data system. This is done by administering surveys to stakeholders. The surveys measure the nine DAAS Index parameters by allowing the actual stakeholders to assess their value in a systematic way. These scores are captured and analyzed, then reviewed with key stakeholders for accuracy and greater contextualization. The DAAS score can then be refined and fully contextualized before it is reported, distributed, and made available in application inventory systems across the enterprise.

This is not just about implementation, but maintenance as well. It is an ongoing process that never ends in a disciplined organization—a continuous improvement cycle. The DAAS Index should be revisited on an ongoing basis—at regular intervals and before making major outlays on IT systems—to ensure it remains up to date. Revisiting the DAAS Index on a periodic basis, such as annually or even biannually—in a fast-moving digital world will keep large and complex enterprises more controllable.

This is only a brief overview of a very complicated topic. Creating, administering, and analyzing the stakeholder surveys must be done by experts to ensure that measurements are made accurately and interpreted properly. For this, you will need an expert. You should only collaborate with partners that are licensed to deliver the DAAS Index. Alternatively, companies may work with technology-services firms who are licensed to deliver the DAAS Index in your geography. For an updated list of licensed firms, agencies, and consultants, please visit the website: www.thebilliondollarbyte.com.

This is especially important because Claritysquare Technology is continuously refining these steps in response to changing technology and business landscapes. We will continue to refine and improve them over time and hope to be able to automate the process in the future.

What the DAAS Index Can Do for You and Your Company

The DAAS Index is an invaluable tool for making sense of today's complex data ecosystems. Operating a large company without using the DAAS Index will soon be as impossible as surfing the Internet without a modern search engine. Understanding the relative value of your data systems is not negotiable in the age of big data. A tool like the DAAS Index is so badly needed in the enterprise world that, as such tools begin to enjoy wider adoption, using them won't be so much of an advantage as not using them will be a handicap.

Without a way to measure the value of your data systems, there is no way to judge the effectiveness of IT investments or decisions. Companies that understand the value of their data are able to make better business decisions. Understanding the value of your systems allows you to invest in the right systems. With the DAAS Index, companies can be sure they are putting their dollars into systems that create true value; they can be sure they are investing in those data assets that are truly returning enterprise value to the company and its stakeholders.

This is key to implementing an effective data strategy. Companies must understand the relative value of their systems in order to structure and leverage them accordingly. As discussed previously, there are three stages of data maturity, in the journey toward creating value through data: data serves the purpose, data as a capability, and data as an asset. By allowing for objective measurement, the DAAS Index allows greater control in the execution of each step. The DAAS Index is effectively a measure of how well data systems deliver on the data strategy. The data strategy is tightly coupled with the business strategy in the Digital Age.

This puts executives back in control of their companies. Good CEOs are strong leaders with clear visions for their companies, but they must be able to see clearly to act upon those visions. Today's business leaders need a tool to make sense of their increasingly complex data ecosystems so that they can make sound business decisions and lead with *clear vision*. In practical terms, this comes down to making the right investments and business decisions. Business leaders will never be able to do that unless they can be confident that they are making the right investments.

With the DAAS Index, they finally have a tool that allows them to actually *know* that their data strategy, an increasingly important part of the business strategy, is delivering true economic value. The DAAS Index provides them with the ability to quantify, measure, control, and monitor information or data-related investments through the use of a simple index. The DAAS Index empowers them with the necessary controls to make the right decisions consistently. Best of all, enterprise value is delivered more effectively and frequently. With the DAAS Index, business leaders can be confident in both their decisions and investments in information-management and data-management programs. Ultimately, this allows business leaders to take control of their own enterprise destiny.

CHAPTER 11

SETTING UP YOUR TEAM MEMBERS TO WIN WITH DATA

"The team with the best players wins."
—**Jack Welch**, Former Chairman and CEO of General Electric

The world is experiencing an unprecedented rate of civilizational change. The interdependency of the global economy allows macroeconomic crises to sweep quickly across regions, or the entire globe. Political upheaval spreads easily and seems near constant. Volatility is the new normal. Technology now outpaces our ability to regulate, litigate, and adjust to the changes it brings.

This acceleration of change is felt acutely in the business world. Technology is creating new opportunities for winners while leaving a trail of losers in its wake. Disruption is the name of the game. As digital companies have upended one industry after another, traditional companies are struggling to keep pace, not only with changing technology, but also with the changing business landscape. Traditional companies are operating in business environments that look nothing like the ones in which they once thrived.

In my experience, the primary thing holding traditional companies back in the Digital Age is their business culture. The business culture of traditional companies is just that—*traditional*. Companies that found success with traditional business models often resist change. When things get rough, they look to the past for example. This can blind legacy companies to the possibilities, and necessities, of the future. Their problem isn't the change itself so much as their inability to adapt to change and reinvent themselves.

Traditional companies must not let past successes blind them to the future unfurling before them. What made traditional companies great in their heyday wasn't their business model, per se. There is no one-size-fits-all perfect business model. The perfect business model is one optimized for present conditions. What made traditional companies succeed was their ability to develop and adopt the right business model for their time and situation. If a company sticks around long enough, as successful companies do, that time will come and go. The old business model that once worked so well may no longer produce the desired results.

If Jack Welch were still driving a traditional company today, he would likely do so with the same guiding philosophy that made General Electric a winner, rising in value by 4,000 percent under two decades of his tenure. Welch's message was always loud and clear: "Keep Learning!" This was his guiding principle. Keep learning. Take new ideas seriously. Be open to change. Remain innovative.

What Jack Welch likely wouldn't do is run General Electric the same way today as he did in the 1980s. He would not cling to an outdated business model that no longer works in the Digital Age. Legacy companies did not succeed because they had the perfect business model. They succeeded because they had the optimal business model for the time. However, an openness to reinvention and a "can do" attitude, the things that actually made successful legacy companies great, will still serve them in the Digital Age if they are willing to reinvent themselves and adjust their business models.

This ethos of innovation, not their old business model, is what legacy companies must hew close to if they hope to win in today's world. Companies that want to survive in today's data-driven, globalized business world must update their business models to reflect the situation on the ground. Now that the pace of change is so quick, today's companies must be in a constant state of reinvention in which they are always reconsidering their business strategy, data strategy, and people strategy.

Much of this book has been focused on data strategy and its relationship to business strategy. In previous chapters, we covered the idea that business models and data strategies must be person-centric. This is because enterprises are made up of individuals. All organizations and enterprises are simply a group of people coming together to create value and do work.

At the end of the day, it is the collective effort of individuals that drives enterprise. Macroeconomics is theory. Microeconomics is praxis. When economic crisis sweeps the globe, it is not the "business community" that must react and adapt. It is individual companies, individual executives, individual entrepreneurs, and individual employees that must come together to steer their own ships.

This makes it incumbent upon companies to have a people strategy integrated into their business model. As we have said before, the business model and business strategy, as well as the data strategy, must be person-centric. The best technology won't cut it; companies need the best people in leadership roles where they can use technology appropriately to win.

Winning is what all enterprises want and need. It is what public companies are bound to do in the form of returning shareholder profits.

There is nothing wrong with winning. When companies win, everyone wins. Winning companies don't take from the economy when they produce a profit; they give back. Winning companies drive up the stock market. Winning companies improve everyone's retirement portfolios. Winning companies pay taxes. Winning companies provide jobs and careers and better lifestyles for all. Winning companies volunteer and engage in philanthropy. Winning companies power the economy and bring prosperity to all.

When companies win, society wins. Owners win. Employees win. Shareholders and other stakeholders win. Everyone wins when companies do well because we all enjoy their products and revenue streams. When companies lose, we all lose. Profits and earnings go down. The stock market performs lower. People are laid off from their jobs. Society is worse off.

This is all felt so acutely by individuals because companies are literally made up of the people who have a stake in them. We call these stakeholders. This includes not just owners and shareholders, but also employees, partners, investors, suppliers, vendors, and the customers who depend on products and services. Companies make up the economy that supports all of us. All boats rise together. A healthy economy and society is driven by solid, successful companies made up of many individuals with a vested stake in their success.

Finding the Right People

Companies operating in the Digital Age, especially legacy companies, must ask themselves, *Do we have the right people in place to steer this ship in this age of landmines, hidden icebergs, and turbulent currents?*

Jack Welch's mantra has always been to focus on people, teamwork, and profits. This is because he understands the relationship between all three. Every enterprise is a concerted effort to create value. It is people coming together through teamwork to create value that makes a successful company. The most successful companies are those that create massive value. In both cases, this value is delivered by people for people.

Good companies invest in their people. Companies need the *right* people. Putting together a successful company requires putting together successful teams. Enterprises are merely teams—and teams of teams. The role of upper leadership is to assemble teams with the right combinations of competencies. Trusting in high-value people is how good companies consistently achieve better outcomes.

Unfortunately, finding the right people has never been harder. Skill sets are becoming more technical and specialized. Matching tech people to tech jobs is difficult when skill sets and job descriptions are so specific. HR departments and even boardrooms don't understand what it is they are hiring for when it comes to IT in the digital age.

Recruiting new talent is especially difficult for traditional companies, whose leadership may not always understand the technology they are using. This can create an environment that is unappealing to technical workers. Many of them are easily lured to the digital companies of the new economy.

The Digital Natives have the advantage here. Not only are they flush with cash to invest in technology workers, they also have built a culture that values technical people. The Digital Natives succeeded by assembling the right people to create new technology platforms and products. They would not be where they are without the right people.

On the other hand, traditional companies started off behind the curve. They rose to prominence before the Digital Age. Not only their teams, but also their hiring practices, predate the Digital Era. This does not mean they cannot assemble teams with the right combination of competencies and skills. It simply means that they must actively do so now. They can hire people with these skills. They can retrain current people. Good people are good people. There is no need to let them go when you can simply teach them new skills.

This is why the business culture must change. Management, HR, and leadership must change the way they recruit and how they train and retain talent. Value should be placed on those who create value. There are no greater creators of value in the digital world than those who can harness data as a capability and asset.

These are the people in whom traditional companies must invest. While companies must invest in all types of crucial people, an extra investment should be made in businesspeople who understand data. This is the age of data. The businesspeople of the future will be those who excel in both traditional business skills and technical skills.

Enter the Datapreneur

In the Digital Age, an appropriate data strategy is an essential component to a business strategy. Developing a data strategy is no longer optional for "winning" enterprises. This is the age of big data. The most successful enterprises will be those who have people able to harness the power of data.

This is why a "person-centric" business model and data strategy are so important. Companies must *work* with data—meaning they must have data *workers*. However, what winning companies need is not an army of analyst drones, "code monkeys," or other low-value technical skills. Winning companies need people who take initiative to harness the power of data for value creation. They need value creators who know the organization, systems, processes and data.

We call these people "datapreneurs" because, as the name suggests, they are entrepreneurial with data. Datapreneurs don't just work with data. They create value with data. They strategize with data. They display leadership and initiative. They define and redefine their own roles as necessary like any other entrepreneur. They look for ways to unlock new value with data through increased revenue, improved compliance, and greater efficiency.

Datapreneurs are uniquely positioned, by way of their twenty-first century skill sets, to create value by leveraging data to make smarter business decisions. This makes them next-level business strategists. For example, traditional strategists may try to increase revenue by increasing customer retention. They know this is a good thing, but may not know how best to accomplish the goal. They have little to go on besides intuition and past experience. These things are of value, but making decisions based on past experience can blind decision makers to changes in the market or industry and there is no way for them to know if their intuition is actually right.

Datapreneurs have the advantage of having accurate information and data-driven insights when making decisions. Rather than simply seeking to increase customer retention, a datapreneur might first collect and analyze data to determine the value delivered by different types of customers. This would allow them to improve efficiency by applying resources toward verified high-value customers. They could also create even more extra value by identifying and letting go of customers who cause losses. For example, if they identify a population group that is not interested in a particular product, they could save the company money by cutting fruitless marketing spending on a hopeless demographic.

There are countless ways that data can be used strategically to improve business processes and update business models. This is especially true for traditional companies. They have more room for improvement than the Digital Natives. The Digital Natives are already optimized, which is why they have already achieved such high valuations. Most legacy companies are now operating inefficiently precisely because they aren't extracting the full value of their data. The upside of this is that they have plenty of room for improvement.

Traditional companies can optimize all facets of their business through better use of data. Data can help companies make better investments and smarter outlays. Data can increase efficiency. Data can improve timing. There are no limits to the way data can return shareholder value—but companies need trained data professionals in leadership roles to unlock this value or leaders trained in data skills.

Leading with Data

Leadership is central to datapreneurship. Entrepreneurs create value from nothing by forming and driving enterprises. Datapreneurs must be similarly entrepreneurial in their use of data. They do not simply accomplish assignments or tasks. They take ownership of their responsibilities. Through the use of data and insights, they identify innovative solutions to the task at hand.

Datapreneurs do not necessarily hold formal leadership positions, though many will. Datapreneurship is not about a particular role or title. They may be on the board or senior executives. They may simply be experts adept in creating data assets that contribute to the value of the company, just as entrepreneurs add value to business ventures. What is key is not that they are technical, but that they are people who drive new value using data, processes and technologies. They are entrepreneurial first and technical if required.

Whatever role they fill, datapreneurs display leadership qualities. They take initiative. They are self-driven. They know how to influence people and business policy. They take responsibility for creating economic value through data. They rally all available people, processes, and technologies to create new value through data and technology. They show financial discipline and understanding, and are outcome oriented. They understand that, at the end of the day, what matters most are results. They are problem solvers who use data to achieve business goals.

To do this, they must understand more than the latest technology. Although datapreneurs are generally technically adept, they are not necessarily technical minded people. They are technology aware, strategic businesspeople. They must understand the role of technology in business—and within their *specific* business context. They understand their enterprise's business processes, the relationship between these processes and the business model, the relationship between that business model and the business strategy, and the role of data in bringing everything together. They use data to help seamlessly integrate the business processes, the business model, and the business strategy.

Data is the datapreneurs' toolkit and arsenal, but their method is that of an entrepreneur. They are able to create, pursue, and realize a vision. They operate in an entrepreneurial manner, using a similar method that an entrepreneur would to take a program or project through its entire life cycle:

- Identify opportunity—*to monetize data investment*
- Influence and garner support in the ecosystem
- Raise funding (capital and budget) for the effort
- Build a team to create and deliver the value proposition
- Scale out the proposition to create more lasting value

These are the same things that any entrepreneur would do. The difference is that datapreneurs are able to improve all of these processes by using data. They can cut through the ambiguity and unprecedented challenge surrounding today's business climate and restore clarity about the business context. They identify opportunities to monetize data investments and then follow through on those investments by laying the groundwork, raising funds, building a team, and ultimately implementing the project and bringing it to scale.

But Where Are All the Datapreneurs?

There is no forgoing the datapreneur in the Digital Age. In order to win in today's business climate, companies need people who can leverage data to improve upon the business model and business strategy. They need people who can use data to develop actionable insight and intelligence. This is the role of the datapreneur, and today's large companies need many of them working in a variety of capacities.

For traditional companies, attracting datapreneurs is a tall order, but it can be done. The Digital Natives have the advantage here. Datapreneurs are drawn to the Digital Natives because they are companies that, by their very nature, value data and tech. Young, entrepreneurial tech people idealize the founders of Google, Facebook, Apple, and other digital companies. They trust these companies to value their skill set. And, for young tech people, there is a certain gravitas to be found in working with the Digital Natives that validates their sense of self.

For all of these reasons, datapreneurs are naturally drawn to the Digital Natives and the new economy. This does not mean that they cannot have rewarding careers at traditional companies; it simply means that they may not realize the opportunities available to them at traditional companies.

Traditional companies that want to attract datapreneurs must both offer opportunities to datapreneurs and advertise this fact in everything they do. This means creating a pro-tech, pro-innovation business culture. Traditional companies must provide growth positions to people who have digital skills and leadership ability. Growth is essential to happiness for companies and individuals alike.

Historically, this has not been the case. Traditional companies have not made data of board-level importance. They have not emphasized the value of data and the people who work with it. There are not enough datapreneurs in leadership positions in most traditional companies. This must change if legacy companies hope to attract the high-value digital workers of today.

While attracting datapreneurs is important, traditional companies may also train new datapreneurs from within their own ranks. The legacy staff at any large traditional company is full of potential datapreneurs.

Datapreneurship is not magic. Those with strong leadership qualities and the drive to learn new skills can be retrained and cross-skilled in data and emerging technologies. They can be taught. They can teach themselves if there are incentives to do so.

I have seen this again and again. For example, in 2004 I started consulting with a utility company in the United Kingdom. They hired me to help build a financial data mart. The project was led by Muriel Pearce, a project manager who was nearing retirement. She had many things working against her. She had never delivered a highly technical program like this before. She suffered from a hearing impairment. She was a woman leading a team in the male-dominated business culture. She was also French and the small-town culture of Sussex wasn't always respectful to her.

Despite these disadvantages, Pearce displayed a fierce tenacity and strong leadership skills. She had long ago learned to compensate for any disadvantages. For example, she'd learned to read lips so well that she could engage in fluid conversation without people knowing about her hearing impairment. She used this same ingenuity and can-do spirit to tackle this new technical project. She was not afraid to ask questions, even at the risk of seeming ignorant or incompetent. In fact, she was neither, certainly not the latter. Within a few weeks, she was up to speed and ready to lead a team of technologists with confidence. In less than a year's time, she delivered the project successfully.

Pearce is the kind of person who can be retrained into a datapreneur. She showed competence, initiative, drive, assurance, and the will to get the job done. She transformed herself into a person capable of leading a technical team.

This is not a fluke, and while Pearce is exceptional, she is by no means unique. This kind of transformation is repeatable. Anyone can be trained to work with emerging technologies. Give the right people the tools to harness data, and they will learn to use them. You simply have to create a culture that encourages and rewards employee growth, initiative, and innovation. Do this, and you will nurture new datapreneurs.

Enterprises should not be scared to give their best people the empowerment, independence, and autonomy they need to act as leaders, whatever their roles. All workers should be managers of themselves. Workers who cannot self-manage and take ownership over their roles are either the wrong workers or are filling roles that shouldn't even exist. Traditional companies need to let go of the reigns and stop micromanaging. They need to attract entrepreneurial people and trust them to help define their roles.

The role of the board and upper management is not to be micromanagers. Instead, the board and top management should work to create teams with the right competencies and create an environment friendly to initiative and self-improvement. Innovation is what happens on the ground when good people are allowed to take initiative. There is no better management than self-management and this starts one person at a time.

This is the path to innovation. Build good teams and don't hobble them. Don't smother them. Don't make them hate their work or feel stagnant in their roles. Datapreneurs think outside the box and will create value if you allow them to do so. They create platforms, not structures. They create value, not bureaucracies. They use the best data and tech to achieve the business goals you set. Build the kinds of teams you can trust and then set them free.

This is the new business culture that traditional companies need to foster in order to attract and nurture the datapreneurs who will create new value and help close the gap between the business strategy and the data strategy. The data strategy is part of the business strategy and it affects all business processes. There should be datapreneurs in the boardroom, on senior leadership, and managing projects and tasks at every level of the enterprise.

Companies that want to win in today's business climate must be ready to reinvent themselves, their business culture, and business model. The Digital Natives succeeded not by virtue of being digital. If that were the case, Pets.com and the other Web 1.0 companies would still be with us today. The digital companies that have shown staying power (e.g., Google, Amazon.com, Facebook, etc.) have done so by creating a culture of innovation and reinvention. Legacy companies that want to keep pace must do the same.

But companies cannot reinvent themselves without knowing the optimal ways to do so and identifying the right timing. This is why datapreneurs are so crucial. They are uniquely positioned to guide companies through the endless cycle of transformation and evolution. They will keep your company from stagnating if you offer them opportunities. Nurture the datapreneurs, and they will nurture your company.

CHAPTER 12

HOW YOU CAN TURN BIG DATA INTO GOOD PROFITS

"A business is simply an idea to make other people's lives better."
—**Sir Richard Branson**, Founder of Virgin Group

All enterprises exist to turn a profit. Owners found companies with hopes for success and wealth. When companies go public, they promise, and make it their mission, to return profit to shareholders. Employees understand that promotions and raises depend on their employer's success. Profit is fundamental to an enterprise. Without profit, no enterprise can succeed. Without successful enterprises, no one succeeds. Our modern economy hinges upon the success of the companies that comprise it. Profit is good.

However, not *all* profits are good. Profit is only good when it improves people's lives and makes the world a better place. Illegal narcotics cartels make huge profits. According to *International Business*

Times, the United States' illegal-narcotics industry grosses between $400 billion and $500 billion annually, perhaps as much as $750 billion. The global markets are even larger. Furthermore, the illegal-narcotics industry enjoys huge profit margins. They are making a killing in profit, but they do so by literally killing people and selling dangerous products that put their customers' health at risk. They make this huge profit by meeting a real market demand, but in doing so, they make the world a worse place for everyone. This is bad profit.

Companies should strive for what businessman Charles Koch calls "good profit." These are profits that improve lives and make the world a better place. In my opinion, a better world is one in which people come together to solve the world's problems. A better world is one in which pharmaceutical companies develop a cure for every disease. A better world is one in which the agriculture industry produces food for all. A better world is one in which companies provide necessities and luxuries while also providing well-paying jobs so that people can afford these items. A better world is one in which we can all do meaningful work that makes the world a better place in some small or big way.

This is not some utopian dream. This is the forward march of the modern economy, fueled by technology and human innovation. Through the creation of good profit, companies create better lives for all people: customers, clients, employees, partners, suppliers, shareholders, or some combination of the aforementioned. Producing good profit—and only good profit—is how companies succeed, win, and do good in the world.

The key here is *doing* good. The world is not changed by thinking and talking alone. Action is the sole driver of change. Action is what ultimately leads to more good profit. Words and messaging, the articulation of ideas, these things matter—but only if they eventually lead to real action. Action drives results. Action actually shapes reality. If those actions are right, timely, and relevant, they will lead companies to good profit and growth of the world economy.

The modern economy is one of the greatest gifts mankind has bestowed upon itself. The economy has brought us abundance, science, progress, modern medicine, technology, and everything modern man holds dear. This only improves year upon year and generation upon generation. Each new generation is the greatest generation ever because it builds upon what came before it. The returns of technology and progress are cumulative, progressive, and rapidly accelerating.

Technology is perhaps the greatest driver of growth and good profit because it allows the world to better serve all causes. Technology not only makes the world a better place, it also makes it easier for others to make the world a better place. This makes me grateful and proud to be a technologist in this age of unprecedented change and forward progress.

Technology creates good profit in a number of ways. Technology helps us produce better returns on investment. It allows us to be more efficient, at work and at home, so that we can spend more time with loved ones. Technology improves health-care delivery and the battle against disease outbreaks, improving public health. Technology is democratizing education and the workplace. Technology is affording people lasting digital preservation of arts, culture, and histories on a scale never seen.

Technology brings people together from around the globe—friends and family, as well as strangers—effectively shrinking the world through greater integration. Technology allows us to work less while producing more. We can telecommute to save time. We can conference from across the globe. We can conduct business across oceans and national lines. The free flow of culture and political ideas no longer knows bounds. This has improved billions of lives.

Technology is allowing us to take better care of our planet and reverse the damage we have done to our environment. Technology affords businesses new ways of conducting business and enables new capabilities. For example, cognitive technologies that simulate human reasoning and perceptual skills have given traditional businesses entirely new capabilities that enable organizations to break currently existing constraints related to speed, cost, and quality. This was unthinkable a few short years ago!

And, of course, technology has created monetary profit for enterprises, their employees, and their shareholders that allows more people more personal freedom and the means and resources to pursue their dreams. Technology has leveled the playing field in many industries and, now more than ever, talent and skill are what drive individuals and enterprises to the top. Technology has given us leisure. Technology allows individuals and organizations to pursue goals and find purpose. Technology allows us to explore and test boundaries. Technology allows us to realize our full potential, which is unbounded in the Digital Age.

In short, technology produces good profit.

Or, at least, it can—and it should. Technology also has the potential to create negative profit that exploits the environment and workers. Technology can enslave us, chaining us to our work devices. Technology can drive us to work eighty-hour weeks year round to make more use of the powerful emerging technologies we have developed. Technology can keep us chasing gadgets and shiny new things. Technology can allow us to spy on each other and violate our enshrined and designated rights. Technology can detract from our life as much as, or more than, it can augment it if we allow this to happen.

This is a world I would neither want to create nor live in. A world in which technology enslaves us or is used to create profit through ill-begotten gains is a world in which the return is not worth the cost. Even if bad profit produces a monetary return, the total return might be negative once you factor in the reduced quality of life, environmental degradation, worker exploitation, and more.

Thankfully, it doesn't have to be this way. The realization of such a world is not why I became a proponent of technology. On the contrary, my goal is to enable and empower companies to use technology to pursue good profit, and good profit *only*. Each and every individual and company can achieve this goal, though it is incumbent upon the entire business community to do so. As citizens and businesspeople, we must commit to using technology for the greater good, even as we chase profit.

The Five Tenets of Good Profit for the Digital Age

But how do companies achieve good profit with technology?

This starts by creating a data-centric business culture based on good profit. Boardrooms, senior leadership, and owners must create a business culture that strives to use technology that not only drives value creation, but also good profit. The best minds in business have mastered value creation, but have not done enough to place an emphasis on good profit.

Charles Koch is the preeminent thinker on this matter. In his book, *Good Profit*, Charles Koch laid out a road map that is part of his Market-Based Management® system for developing better corporate governance through free-market ideas. Koch named five "dimensions," or lenses, through which to view an organization. They are: vision (i.e., allocating capabilities to best create value), virtues and talent (i.e., building teams based on value over raw talent), knowledge processes (i.e., tracking data around value creation), decision rights (i.e., getting the right people in the right roles), and incentives (i.e., providing proper rewards based on long-term value creation). These five dimensions, according to Koch, are integral to value creation.

Koch developed a strong framework for helping enterprises create value and good profit, but his framework does not allow adequate attention to the circumstances of the Digital Age and the explosion of big data. The five dimensions only explicitly acknowledge the role of data when discussing "knowledge processes," but in today's business world, data must play a role in every single thing that enterprises do.

To that end, we have developed a different plan for companies that want to create good profit in the Digital Age. We suggest Five Tenets of Good Profit for the Digital Age that focus not only on value creation, but also on the role of data assets in every step of that value creation. This is the best way to create good profit in today's digital, data-centric business environment.

Our Five Tenets of Good Profit for the Digital Age are laid out in the chart below.

In the Digital Age, companies need to leverage data to improve all processes (i.e., tenet 1). Data strategy should be baked into the company vision and utilized as a core asset and resource. Data analysis should govern and guide all business processes that any enterprise conducts. Data must be central to the business model and the company's overall vision.

Recruitment and retention of talent should use data to improve HR practices, while placing a special focus on both virtue and talent in order to attract people with the right skills and leadership qualities (i.e., tenet 2). Companies must also create a culture of contribution in which employees are trusted to have personal ownership over their own purview and allowed autonomy and decision rights (i.e., tenet 3). These tenets are key to attracting and nurturing datapreneurs.

Companies may further maximize the contribution of individuals by basing compensation on value creation (i.e., tenet 4). Compensating by the hour or with a defined salary without generous bonus options is an Industrial Age mind-set that trades labor for monetary compensation. This worked when labor produced a fixed return, but in the Digital Age, there is no limit to value creation. Technology allows productivity to scale up without limit. Ideally, there should be no hard limit on compensation, just as there is no hard limit on value creation. This keeps people motivated to do better and creates an environment where they have the autonomy to do so.

Finally, companies should create a giving culture that creates a systematic process for improving the lives of the less fortunate (i.e., tenet 5). This doesn't have to be "philanthropy." Enterprises are not, at their core, philanthropic endeavors. They operate under a profit motive. This does not preclude enterprises from operating by a strict moral code that strives to profit only by doing good. Thankfully, doing good is profitable. Consumers generally want to purchase things that make their own lives better, as well as those of others. Companies can improve the lives of the less fortunate simply by offering them needed products and services at a fair value through fair practices and fair contributions.

How Can Big Data Enable the Pursuit of Good Profit?

With these Five Tenets, companies can create a business culture that enables good profits in the Digital Age by fully leveraging data. Data is a powerful tool for businesses. It is also a powerful tool in the pursuit of good profit. Data allows businesses **to make good and timely decisions in a systematic and scientific manner.** Without data, businesses would have nothing to go on but sheer intuition.

Timing is key to good business decisions. The right decision must come at the right time. There is a right time to launch a new product or retire an old product line. There is a right time to hire new staff members. There is a right time to reorganize, take a company public, engage in a merger or acquisition, sell off or rebrand the company, and to make any other business decision.

By collecting, processing, and analyzing data on an ongoing basis, companies have a means of assessing their business decisions with confidence. Data holds information and insights that can guide companies to make the right decision at the right time. This is the power of big data in business. It is also the power of so-called "small data."

Small data is simply the full leverage of data at a company that may not be operating at the scale of the biggest Digital Natives, such as Google or Facebook. Big data doesn't have to be "big" in the way we normally think of it. All data deals with people, products, and processes. Both small and large companies deal with all of these things. All companies should be leveraging data fully, whether they are working with data from billions, millions, thousands, or mere hundreds of people. Companies that win and profit, no matter their size, are those that fully leverage data to make the best decisions at the right time.

Big companies and small companies, traditional companies and Digital Native new-economy companies, any and all companies should all approach data in the same way. Traditional companies and smaller or newer enterprises should not allow the term "big data" to intimidate them. The various big-data technology vendors that are worth their salt all do the same thing: They help companies understand their business model and the business processes that comprise that model. They help companies implement systems that ensure that data from all business processes is captured, cleansed, standardized, organized, and made available for systematic and timely decision making through analytics and visualizations.

Companies can use the information and insights gleaned from these tools to develop a business model optimized to the current business context. This is best done by observing the data generated by the processes from the business model. When companies understand their data in the context of their business circumstances, they can adapt the business model to the data it produces.

Earlier in this book, we discussed a business-model map that looked at the business model in the context of data. The business model of data is again pictured on the next page.

All businesses, no matter their industry, will be better equipped to pursue the creation of value partnerships and relationships, manage resources and channels, increase efficiency, decrease costs, and optimize revenue streams by making good use of existing technology and emerging technology related to analytics.

This simply requires that the right data-driven strategies be put in place. This includes an optimal business strategy, a sound data strategy, and a people strategy that considers data and technology. In the end, data strategy comes down to people, processes, and technologies. Data can connect the three dots—people, processes, and technology. Companies just need a bulletproof data strategy that realizes the full and complete value of data. This is the Three-Step Data Maturity Mantra we discussed earlier in this book:

- Data Serves the Purpose.
- Data As A Capability.
- Data As An Asset.

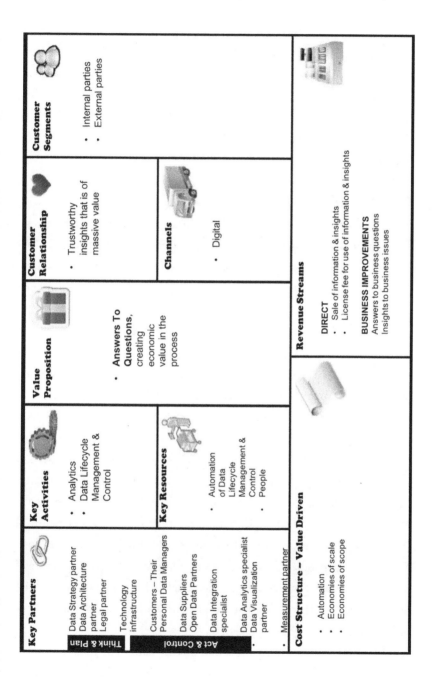

Customer Segments
- Internal parties
- External parties

Customer Relationship
- Trustworthy insights that is of massive value

Channels
- Digital

Value Proposition
- **Answers To Questions,** creating economic value in the process

Key Activities
- Analytics
- Data Lifecycle Management & Control

Key Resources
- Automation of Data Lifecycle Management & Control
- People

Key Partners

Think & Plan
- Data Strategy partner
- Data Architecture partner
- Legal partner
- Technology infrastructure
- Customers – Their Personal Data Managers

Act & Control
- Data Suppliers
- Open Data Partners
- Data Integration specialist
- Data Analytics specialist
- Data Visualization partner
- Measurement partner

Revenue Streams

DIRECT
- Sale of information & insights
- License fee for use of information & insights

BUSINESS IMPROVEMENTS
Answers to business questions
Insights to business issues

Cost Structure – Value Driven
- Automation
- Economies of scale
- Economies of scope

When data is leveraged to deliver value through this three-step strategy, companies are better positioned to win and accumulate good profit. The right datapreneurs, armed with the right tools, such as the Data as an Asset (DAAS) Index and an optimized IT infrastructure, can realize the full value of their data.

As has been proven again and again, the full value of that data is quite high.

The Billion Dollar Byte

Business data is simply the trail left behind from business processes. These business processes are centered on people. There are processes for handling customers, employees, partners, vendors, and more. Business data tracks people. Once enriched, this data provides information and insights into the behavior and motivations of these people.

Collectively, these 'persons' make up, drive, and support the enterprise. This is why the data about them is so important. They are the heart of any enterprise. This is why companies must embrace person-centric data strategies. To be truly data-centric is to be person-centric. Data cannot be fully monetized unless the data strategy is person-centric in every aspect. Companies must strive to use person-centric data to better understand the people who are relevant to the business model.

Do not lose sight of the fact that data is about people. Customers, partners, owners, employees, managers, shareholders, and all other stakeholders are people first. This is crucial to understanding their behavior. Investments into data should always be focused on understanding people. Companies must understand the wants, needs, preferences, biases, and actions of the people who are relevant to their business model. This is both necessary and completely possible. The information is right there in the data.

There is no overstating the value of this data. The most valuable data is that which defines a person. This data, once it is refined, is highly valuable. I call this data the **Billion Dollar Byte.** Once collected, processed, and made into consumable information in the form of visualizations and analytics, this data provides actionable intelligence and insights. The Billion Dollar Byte contains information about people relevant to the company—be they customers, shareholders, employees, or any other stakeholder. Collect this data, analyze and enrich it, protect it vigorously, and use it to draw valuable insight that can help you optimize your business model and business strategy.

Companies have always collected data and used it to draw insights. The difference today, in the Digital Age, is that emerging technologies now allow enterprises to collect, process, and analyze this data in much greater detail and on a massive scale. The collection and enrichment processes can also be automated. They can be employed systematically across the globe at all levels of the business. The data collection can be built into the business processes so that it is all automatic and ordered. Data is still data, but our ability to work with it has increased by orders of magnitude in a very short time.

This is where emerging big-data tools and technologies come into play. These are not the be-all and end-all of big-data technology. They are only tools. Buying the latest and greatest tools means nothing if they are not employed properly. These tools only return real value when they are part of a greater data strategy embedded within the business model. These tools are only useful when companies put them in the hands of skilled people (i.e., datapreneurs) who can make the most of them. Again, real value creation lies at the intersection of people, processes, and technology.

Pulling It All Together

In the hands of the right people, emerging data technologies absolutely can unlock great value for companies, especially traditional companies that are not yet fully leveraging their data. Datapreneurs allowed autonomy and access to these tools can create not just big profit—but also, big *good* profit. You need the right people with the right technology working with data to put the right processes in place. That is how companies can "connect the dots" and implement a winning data strategy.

Today, all companies should be operating with a strategic intent appropriate to the Digital Age of big data. This will allow them to pull all of the available technologies and infrastructure together in order to create a winning data strategy.

This ultimately comes down to three things:

- Commoditize the technology infrastructure
- Industrialize data integration
- Pervade reporting, analytics, and visualization throughout the organization

Operating with strategic intent in this way allows companies to bring their whole IT infrastructure together into one model, pictured on the next page.

This graphic pulls together all of the subjects of this book. This is the blueprint for companies that want to implement a winning data strategy and data infrastructure. By organizing data better and managing it properly across the entire data life cycle, from collection through process and into consumption, companies can unlock new value that will lead to good profits.

This is a holistic approach to data strategy. Companies must collect data carefully. They must better organize their data across its entire life cycle. They must use the DAAS Index to properly manage and monitor data. They must invest heavily in consumption technologies, such as visualization and analytics, in order to extract information from the data. They must secure that information properly. They must use that information to develop actionable insights and then execute on those

PULLING IT ALL TOGETHER - BIG DATA FOR GOOD PROFIT

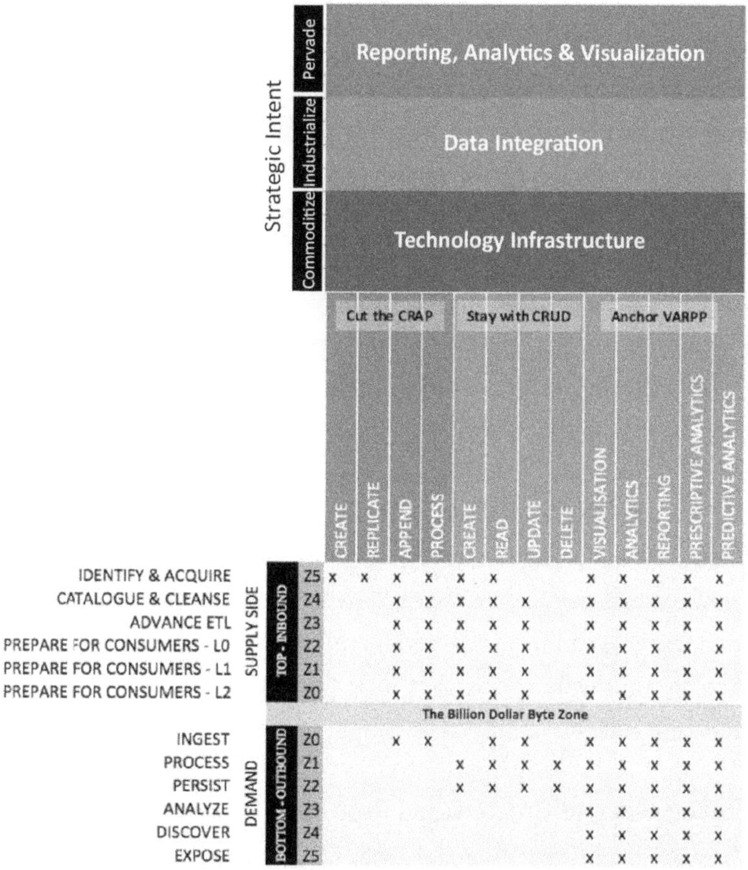

		Cut the CRAP				Stay with CRUD				Anchor VARPP				
		CREATE	REPLICATE	APPEND	PROCESS	CREATE	READ	UPDATE	DELETE	VISUALISATION	ANALYTICS	REPORTING	PRESCRIPTIVE ANALYTICS	PREDICTIVE ANALYTICS
IDENTIFY & ACQUIRE	Z5	x	x	x	x	x	x			x	x	x	x	x
CATALOGUE & CLEANSE	Z4		x	x	x	x	x			x	x	x	x	x
ADVANCE ETL	Z3		x	x	x	x	x			x	x	x	x	x
PREPARE FOR CONSUMERS - L0	Z2		x	x	x	x	x			x	x	x	x	x
PREPARE FOR CONSUMERS - L1	Z1		x	x	x	x	x			x	x	x	x	x
PREPARE FOR CONSUMERS - L2	Z0		x	x	x	x	x			x	x	x	x	x
The Billion Dollar Byte Zone														
INGEST	Z0	x	x			x	x			x	x	x	x	x
PROCESS	Z1					x	x	x	x	x	x	x	x	x
PERSIST	Z2					x	x	x	x	x	x	x	x	x
ANALYZE	Z3									x	x	x	x	x
DISCOVER	Z4									x	x	x	x	x
EXPOSE	Z5									x	x	x	x	x

(Left axis: SUPPLY SIDE / TOP-INBOUND for the top six rows; DEMAND / BOTTOM-OUTBOUND for the bottom six rows. Vertical axis at far left: Strategic Intent — Commoditize, Industrialize, Pervade. Top horizontal bands: Reporting, Analytics & Visualization; Data Integration; Technology Infrastructure.)

actions. They need to have datapreneurs in place to work with the data and use it to amend the business processes and business model proactively and in a timely manner.

This is a tall order. Thankfully, companies do not have to go it alone. There are technology vendors and specialist consulting firms that can help. There are many analytics vendors willing to bid on projects. They can help companies commoditize and industrialize their technology infrastructure and integrate data into their business model for value creation. They can help companies manage the life cycle of data and strategize their data usage. They can help companies develop a data strategy for the Digital Age.

For their part, companies must first be ready to undertake this journey. They must adopt the right mind-set and develop the right attitude. They must remain open-minded and ready to execute the right actions—even if they deviate from the current business model. This is an especially hard pill for traditional companies to swallow, but they must be ready to abandon old business models and modify business processes. If the data indicates a better way, companies must be ready to chart a new course. After crunching all of that data by investing heavily in analytics and visualization, companies must be prepared to go where the data tells them.

This is not an overnight event. Commitment to being data-centric is an ongoing process. Companies must also be willing to measure, monitor, and control outcomes. A commitment to data is a true commitment. Companies must commit to using and trusting data, if it is going to provide solutions to their business problems and lead them to good profit.

Proven Ways to Create Good Profit with Big Data

There are many ways companies can employ big data to produce good profit. There are at least six major ways that good profit can be generated with emerging data technologies:

1. Increased Revenues
2. Reduced Expenditures
3. Profitable Compliance
4. Improved Business Valuation
5. Attraction and Retention of Talent
6. Global Contribution

Increased revenue is the most direct method of increasing profits. Big data allows enterprises to better understand their own businesses and industries through the use of high-quality analytics. Data and the insights it yields can help companies increase sales, enhance revenue streams, and improve product offerings. Increased revenues are a function of the business doing better business. This is especially true when companies employ person-centric analytics to better understand the market, allowing them to maximize revenue by appealing to the right people.

The second most direct way of increasing profits is by reducing expenditures. Data collected on business processes can be used to identify and systematically eliminate inefficiencies. Methods such as process analytics are perfect for this job. Improved efficiency that leads to lower expenditures is a direct way to turn hard-earned revenues into captured profits.

The third way companies can use data to increase profits is by engaging in profitable compliance. Compliance is a major cost. Companies can lose big if they face a fine or are publicly exposed as noncompliant on issues of financial risk, safety, or corporate responsibility. Companies must ensure that all business processes are compliant with regulations. There are often many ways in which companies can comply with regulations. Profitable compliance is when companies find the most efficient and low-cost methods of honestly and fully meeting compliance. Because compliance is managed through business processes, companies have data about their compliance programs that can be used to streamline those processes. Companies should ensure that data and analytics are an integral part of their auditing and compliance programs.

The fourth way in which companies can profit from big data is through a massive increase in their business valuation. Companies achieve higher valuations by putting an emphasis on the pursuit of economic value. Value creation is the pursuit of all enterprises. All business processes should focus on value creation. There are, of course, innumerable ways to do this with big data, such as creating person-centric data practices.

Creating value is not just about what companies do. They must also consider what not to do. Initiatives that don't create value should not be pursued. Companies that want to increase their valuation should abandon activities that don't create economic value. These no- and low-value initiatives can be identified through data analytics.

The fifth way of creating profit with big data is by attracting and retaining talent. To do this, companies must create an ecosystem that not only attracts good people, but also one that encourages them to stay by offering rewards, growth potential, and a good company culture. Companies must reconsider how they manage people. Again, data is your friend here. Companies should employ person-centric analytics for talent management.

Above all, invest in the datapreneur. Companies need people with leadership as well as technical abilities in a variety of roles. Search for ways to train and develop staff to become your datapreneurs. All key people in a company, no matter their role, should receive continuous and relevant development throughout their career.

The sixth way that companies can increase good profits through big data is by contributing to the world. This is what makes profits *good*. When what a company does contributes to the betterment of the world, the profits it produces are good profits. This positive contribution doesn't have to be "synthetically" philanthropic. Companies profit when they truly meet people's wants and needs. This betters the world. And when data is used, it is an example of data bettering the world. This happens all of the time in the age of big data. For example, when a tech company supplies certain analytics to an industry, this betters all of society by contributing to the economy. It is also true that the companies using those analytics are now profiting more, as well as contributing more to society.

This sixth and final method of increasing profits is particularly important because it underpins the way in which profit for companies becomes good profit for societies. This happens all the time and is a function of the kind of strong free-market economy for which Charles Koch and others, including myself, advocate.

CHAPTER 13

GETTING STARTED WITH BIG DATA AND EMERGING TECHNOLOGIES

"Leadership is about making the right decision and the best decision before, sometimes, it becomes entirely popular."
—**Martin O'Malley**, American Politician

The imminent importance of data in the new economy is undeniable. Traditional companies cannot cling to outmoded business models and hope to survive in the Digital Age. They must move away from legacy business models, no matter how successful they were yesterday, and embrace data-driven business models, emerging technologies, and a business culture that is person-centric and nurturing of technology and technologists.

Companies looking to get started on revitalizing their relationship with data must begin by understanding that there is no quick fix. Companies do not develop and implement a data strategy overnight.

They do not build out a new technology infrastructure in a day. They do not rewrite their business model at the drop of a dime. They do not change over all of their business processes at the snap of a finger. A full transformation will take time.

This is an ongoing process. Companies that stay on top are constantly reassessing their business model and data strategy on an ongoing basis. They monitor outcomes and adjust as they go. The new economy is a volatile one. Disruption and change are ongoing. Companies must learn to embrace sustained and ongoing change. Evolution is the only way to stay at the top.

However, it is also possible to achieve significant immediate results. Companies can see instantaneous economic returns by expanding and improving their data analytics. The following is a list of the various types of analytics on which companies can focus in their pursuit of immediate economic value.

- Predictive-sales analytics
- Customer-profitability analytics
- Product-profitability analytics
- Cash-flow analytics
- Value-driver analytics
- Shareholder-value analytics

This is by no means an exhaustive list. There are many ways that a company's analytics can be put to immediate use. This pertains to both big data and small data. Whether you are a large global bank or a Fortune 500 hotel group, you can use analytics to start improving multiple processes right away.

These value-added analytics can be implemented quickly, but they do require effective implementation. Traditional companies especially may lack the integration between IT and the boardroom to make the most of analytics. This requires a change in their approach to data. It will be necessary to understand and reflect your business model accurately along with the key business processes to represent the data footprint accurately and relevantly. As with any major rollout or restructuring, companies really need proven experts to achieve optimum and swift results.

As Chief Data Partner at Claritysquare Technology and Founder of The Data Strategy Lab, I spend every day helping companies understand and formulate strategies to create economic value through the use of data and emerging technologies. We help companies assess their needs in the Digital Age, and develop and implement a data strategy that pursues economic value creation. We help companies in a multitude of ways:

- **Data-Strategy Advisory**
  - o   We consult with companies to develop and implement the optimal data strategy. This includes data-strategy advisory paired with concrete digital-transformation initiatives to carry companies from business case development, architecture, and design through to development and implementation.
  - o   We offer workshops that show companies how to align their business strategy and business model with their new data strategy for immediate new value creation.
- **Big-Data Tools and Technologies**
  - o   There are many technology vendors offering myriad options. It can be hard for company boards and executives to know what tools and technologies are worth investing in.
  - o   We guide companies through the assessment and selection process. Companies don't need the latest or most expensive tools; they need the *right* tools to implement their new data strategy. Companies need tools and technologies that can

handle data across its entire life cycle and tie the different stages of the life cycle to specific business processes.

- **Talent Development**
  - We offer training and people-development programs that will help companies, particularly traditional companies, and HR departments build winning teams by better recruiting, developing, and retaining datapreneurs (i.e., those individuals with the right combination of technical skill sets and leadership qualities).
  - We train sales teams to improve their revenues through the use of data and analytics.
  - We also provide coaching and mentoring for leaders in technology. These workshops will help train and develop the next generation of datapreneurs that will carry your enterprise forward into the Digital Age.

- **The Data as an Asset (DAAS) Index**
  - Companies need a system for assessing the relative value of their digital systems, applications, and data assets in order to properly allocate resources. Our proprietary DAAS Index system is a tool that does just that.
  - The DAAS Index is not just a piece of software you can simply install; it is a system for measuring the relative value of digital assets. We offer implementation advisory to help companies get started with a new way of thinking about the value that data brings.

- **Strategy and Architecture Advisory**
  - Once a data strategy is in place, companies must build out the digital technology infrastructure. There are a number of vendors that can build specific systems, but what companies really need is advisory on how to build technology infrastructure strategically with a holistic

perspective and, more importantly, which is vendor and technology agnostic.

- o We advise companies on:
    - — Data Architecture (e.g., Class-N ODS, a.k.a. data lakes, data warehouses, data marts, operational data stores, etc.)
    - — Technology Architecture
    - — Data Modeling
    - — Enterprise-Data Governance
    - — Data Quality Management
    - — Data-Migration Programs
    - — Master Data-Management Programs
    - — Data-Centric Programs—Assessments and Reviews

How You and Your Organization Can Benefit:

- Training, Seminars, and Workshops
    - o The Datapreneur Series: Developing People for the Digital Age
    - o The Billion Dollar Byte Series—Data Strategy for Companies
- Top-Line Focus
- Bottom-Line Focus
    - o Bits 'n' Bytes Series—Know your data better. See it. Feel it. Act on it.
    - o Advisory and Consulting Services
- Chief Data Partner services to large and complex traditional organizations

No two companies are alike. All companies have different business models and operate in different business environments. However, all enterprises share a few commonalities. This includes both traditional companies and the Digital Natives of the new economy. All companies, regardless of business or size, are best served by developing a value-driven, person-centric data strategy and integrating it into their business model and its business processes. All companies thoroughly benefit from focusing on data-driven value creation. All companies need to nurture datapreneurs and funnel them into leadership roles throughout the enterprise because all companies share the desire to increase economic value and their contribution of good profit.

This book is limited by space. For more information, visit the Billion Dollar Byte book blog at www.thebilliondollarbyte.com.

ABOUT THE AUTHOR

Justhy Deva Prasad (aka D. Justhy) is a leading authority on data strategy, data management and big data analytics. He is a passionate leader, speaker, author, consultant, and the founder of The Data Strategy Lab, Zürich, Switzerland.

Justhy (as he would like to be called) knows both technology and business. A results-oriented practitioner and a pragmatic strategist, he has been serving and delivering value to the global business community for nearly two decades. He has advised Fortune 500 companies and other clients on behalf of IBM Labs, as well as other international consultancies, including his own. He is the founder and Chief Data Partner of Claritysquare Technology, a global consultancy that helps business leaders create economic value through the use and application of data.

While many technology-focused consultancies work primarily with digital companies, Justhy has made it his mission to help longstanding "traditional" legacy enterprises transition into the digital age by adopting the same people- and data-centric approaches employed by today's tech behemoths. He believes there is no reason traditional companies cannot use data to achieve the same astronomic valuations as the world's biggest digital enterprises.

Justhy, an engineer by training, also studied business and marketing at the University of Lincoln, where he earned his MBA, as well as completing a private equity program at the London Business School. A true global citizen, he was born in India and currently resides in Zürich, Switzerland with his wife and children.

FREE RESOURCES FOR THE EXECUTIVE

No.	Resource Description	URL
1	Experian Information Solutions Inc	https://www.edq.com/uk/resources/infographics/the-dawn-of-the-chief-data-officer/
2	IBM	http://www.ibm.com/analytics/us/en/technology/chief-data-officer/

3	The International Society of Chief Data Officers (ISCDO) is the professional society of individuals who serve the role of the Chief Data Officers (CDOs) for their organizations. Their vision is to enable enterprises to derive the maximum value from its information and data assets, to realize the value of data-driven decision-making, and to gain competitive advantage through high-quality information.	http://www.iscdo.org
4	The Data Warehouse Institute	https://tdwi.org/Home.aspx
5	DataPortals.org is the most comprehensive list of open data portals in the world. It is created by a group of leading open data experts from around the world—including representatives from local, regional and national governments, international organizations such as the World Bank, and numerous NGOs.	http://dataportals.org

6	The OD500 Global Network is an international network of organizations that seek to study the use and impact of open data. Coordinated by the Governance Lab (GovLab) the OD500 Global Network enables participating organizations to analyze open data in their country in a manner that is both globally comparative and domestically specific. The OD500 Global Network starts from the assumption that only by mapping the use of open data within and across countries, can new approaches for understanding the economic and social impact of open government data be generated.	http://www.opendata500.com
7	Governing through technology	http://www.thegovlab.org
8	A comprehensive list of 2600+ open data portals around the world	https://www.opendatasoft.com/a-comprehensive-list-of-all-open-data-portals-around-the-world/

9	One of the most effective ways to display development indicators is through graphs and charts. A visual display of data makes comparisons easier and promotes a better understanding of trends. They provide data dashboards on various topics as well as access to all the underlying data through our latest data visualization and sharing application	http://data.worldbank.org/products/tools

10	Google Public Data Explorer—Google Public Data Explorer is a new experimental product designed by Google allowing people to mash up data using line graphs, bar graphs, maps and bubble charts. The visualizations are dynamic, so you can watch them move over time, change topics, highlight different entries and change the scale. Once you have a chart ready, you can easily share it with friends or even embed it on your own website or blog. As of 4/20/2010, Data Explorer contains 58 World Development Indicators.	http://www.google.com

| 11 | Google Public Data Search—Google Public Data Search allows users to perform English search queries for data on Google and instantly see numerical and graphical results. For example, if you search for "gdp of Indonesia," you will see a thumbnail graph at the top of the search results page highlighting Bank data and linking to an interactive chart where you can compare the selected data with other countries around the world. You can also embed these charts in your own website or blog by clicking on the "Link" button in the upper right-hand corner of the chart page. As of 4/20/2010, Google search provides search results for 39 World Development Indicators. | http://www.google.com |

12	The European Data Portal harvests the metadata of Public Sector Information available on public data portals across European countries. Information regarding the provision of data and the benefits of re-using data is also included.	https://www.europeandataportal.eu
13	The Institute for Operations Research and the Management Sciences (INFORMS) is the largest society in the world for professionals in the field of operations research (O.R.), management science, and analytics.	http://analytics-magazine.org
14	First 100 days of a chief data officer	http://www.gartner.com/smarterwithgartner/first-100-days-of-a-chief-data-officer/
15	Book: the case for the chief data officer	http://www.datablueprint.com/thought-leaders/peter-aiken/book-the-case-for-the-cdo/
16	Point of view: Stewarding Data: Why Financial Services Firms Need a Chief Data Officer	https://www.capgemini.com/resources/stewarding-data-why-financial-services-firms-need-a-chief-data-officer

17	Article: The chief data officer's dilemma: CDO role in flux	http://searchdatamanagement.techtarget.com/news/450300878/The-chief-data-officers-dilemma-CDO-role-in-flux
18	Paper: The Data Revolution and Economic Analysis	http://www.nber.org/papers/w19035
19	McKinsey Quarterly	www.mckinsey.com
20	A T Kearney	http://www.atkearney.com/
21	Accenture	http://www.accenture.com/
22	Bain & Company	http://www.bain.com/
23	Booz Allen Hamilton	http://www.boozallen.com/
24	Boston Consulting Group	http://www.bcg.com/
25	Deloitte Consulting	http://www.deloitte.com/
26	Ernst & Young (EY)	http://www.ey.com/
27	IBM BCS	http://www-1.ibm.com/services/us/bcs/html/bcs_index.html
28	KPMG	http://www.kpmg.com/
29	McKinsey & Company	http://www.mckinsey.com/
30	PA Consulting	http://www.paconsulting.com/
31	Price Waterhouse Coopers	http://www.pwc.com/
32	Roland Berger Strategy Consultants	http://www.rolandberger.com/
33	Beye Network	http://www.b-eye-network.com
34	EY Insights	http://www.ey.com/
35	Ernst & Young Center for Board Matters	http://www.ey.com/

36	Dun & Bradstreet	www.dnb.com
37	CACI International Inc	www.caci.com
38	Dunnhumby	www.dunnhumby.com
39	Cognizant Technology	www.cognizant.com
40	Palantir Technology	www.palantir.com

To learn more about how data can work for you, visit www.thebilliondollarbyte.com for a free download of "The Billion Dollar Byte" infographic.

ENDNOTES

Chapter 1: Are You Data Partying Like it's the Nineties or Are You Just Stuck?

1. Michael Hickins, "Social is a Feature, Not a Product," *The Wall Street Journal*, May 23, 2013, http://blogs.wsj.com/cio/2013/05/23/social-is-a-feature-not-a-product/.

2. Clint Boulton, "Airbnb Tops Challenges of Spark Implementation," *The Wall Street Journal*, July 1, 2015, http://blogs.wsj.com/cio/2015/07/01/airbnb-tops-challenges-of-spark-implementation/.

3. Jeff Vance, "Big Data Analytics Overview," Datamation, last modified June 8, 2015, http://www.datamation.com/applications/big-data-analytics-overview.html.

4. Kim S. Nash, "Big Data for Bigger Sales: Thermo Fisher Uses New Tech to Mine Sales Leads," *The Wall Street Journal*, June 29, 2015, http://blogs.wsj.com/cio/2015/06/29/big-data-for-bigger-sales-thermo-scientific-uses-new-tech-to-mine-sales-leads/.

5. Randy Bean, "Big Data Fuels a 'Data First' Movement," *The Wall Street Journal*, June 15, 2015, http://blogs.wsj.com/cio/2015/06/15/big-data-fuels-a-data-first-movement/.

6. Clint Boulton, "Big Data Headed for 'Hellabyte Metric, says Andrew McAfee," *The Wall Street Journal*, October 7, 2013, http://blogs.wsj.com/cio/2013/10/07/big-data-headed-for-hellabyte-metric-says-andrew-mcafee/ .

7. Nick Suh, "Big Data's Hidden Benefit for Corporate IT Data Centers," Information Management Online, last modified July 23, 2015, http://www.information-management.com/news/big-data-analytics/Big-Data-Corporate-IT-Infrastructure-Management-10027281-1.html .

8. Liran Einav and Jonathan Levin, "The Data Revolution and Economic Analysis," The National Bureau of Economic Research, (NBER Working Paper No. 19035), issued May 2013, presented at NBER Innovation Policy and the Economy Conference April 2013, http://www.nber.org/papers/w19035 .

9. Dave Aron, Graham Waller, Lee Weldon, *Flipping to Digital Leadership: The 2015 CIO Agenda*, Gartner, Executive Summary, 2015, https://www.gartner.com/imagesrv/cio/pdf/cio_agenda_execsum2015.pdf.

10. Mark J. Perry, "Fortune 500 Firms in 1955 vs. 2014; 88% are gone, and we're all better off because of that dynamic 'creative destruction,'" AEI Publications, last modified August 18, 2014, http://www.aei.org/publication/fortune-500-firms-in-1955-vs-2014-89-are-gone-and-were-all-better-off-because-of-that-dynamic-creative-destruction/.

11. Charles-Edouard Bouée, "Does Your Company Have a Plan D?" World Economic Forum, last modified February 24, 2016, https://www.weforum.org/agenda/2016/02/radically-digital.

Chapter 2: The Digital Era and the End of the Industrial Age

1. Gilles Babinet, *L'Ère numérique, un nouvel âge de l'humanité*, (Paris : Le Passeur Éditeur, 2014.)
2. "The Data Deluge, » *The Economist*, February 25, 2010, http://www.economist.com/node/15579717.
3. "Jevons paradox," *Wikipedia*, last modified January 27, 2017, https://en.wikipedia.org/wiki/Jevons_paradox.
4. John Gantz and David Reinsel, "The Digital Universe Decade— Are you Ready?" IDC Digital University Study, May 2010. https://www.emc.com/collateral/analyst-reports/idc-digital-universe-are-you-ready.pdf.
5. "Social Media Valuation and the Value of a User," Appraisal Economics Report, 2014, https://www.appraisaleconomics.com/wp-content/uploads/Social-Media-Valuation-and-the-Value-of-a-User.pdf

Chapter 3: If You're Skeptical about Big Data, You're Right

1. Thor Olavsrud, "IDC Says Big Data to Hit $48.6 Billion in 2019," CIO.com, last updated November 11, 2015, http://www.cio.com/article/3004512/big-data/idc-predicts-big-data-spending-to-reach-48-6-billion-in-2019.html.

Chapter 4: Data Creates Enterprise Value, Not Just Jobs

1. Douglas Laney, "Methods for Monetizing Your Data" (webinar, Gartner Webinars, accessed February 10, 2017), https://www.gartner.com/webinar/3098518.
2. Douglas Laney, Mario Faria, Alan D. Duncan, "Seven Steps to Monetizing Your Information Assets," Gartner, updated October 7, 2016, https://www.gartner.com/doc/3151321/seven-steps-monetizing-information-assets.

3. Rachael King, "Analytics Predict Which Patients Will Supper Post-Surgical Infections," CIO Journal, *The Wall Street Journal*, February 11, 2015, http://blogs.wsj.com/cio/2015/02/11/analytics-predict-which-patients-will-suffer-post-surgical-infections/.

4. Rachael King, "AT&T Uses Big Data to Improve Customer Experience," CIO Journal, *The Wall Street Journal*, June 3, 2014, http://blogs.wsj.com/cio/2014/06/03/att-uses-big-data-to-improve-customer-experience/.

5. Clint Boulton, "Auto Insurers Bank on Big Data to Drive New Business," CIO Journal, *The Wall Street Journal*, February 20, 2013, http://blogs.wsj.com/cio/2013/02/20/auto-insurers-bank-on-big-data-to-drive-new-business/.

6. Betsy Atkins, "Big Data and the Board," CIO Journal, *The Wall Street Journal*, April 16, 2015, http://blogs.wsj.com/cio/2015/04/16/big-data-and-the-board/.

7. Randy Bean, "Big Data and the Visionary Power of Change," CIO Journal, *The Wall Street Journal*, May 20, 2014, http://blogs.wsj.com/cio/2014/05/20/big-data-and-the-visionary-power-of-change/.

8. "Bob DeRodes on Garnering Respect as CIO," Deloitte Insights, CIO Journal, *The Wall Street Journal*, August 10, 2015, http://deloitte.wsj.com/cio/2015/08/10/bob-derodes-on-garnering-respect-as-cio/.

9. Clint Boulton, "CIOs Rank Analytics As Top Strategic Priority," CIO Journal, *The Wall Street Journal*, February 6, 2014, http://blogs.wsj.com/cio/2014/02/06/cios-rank-analytics-as-top-strategic-priority/.

10. Michael Hickins, "Companies Engage in 'Hidden Market for Data Monetization,'" CIO Journal, *The Wall Street Journal*, January 23, 2014, http://blogs.wsj.com/cio/2014/01/23/companies-engage-in-hidden-market-for-data-monetization/.

11. Rachael King, "Data Helps Drive Lower Mortality Rate at Kaiser," CIO Journal, *The Wall Street Journal*, December 5, 2013, http:// blogs.wsj.com/cio/2013/12/05/data-helps-drive-lower-mortality-rate-at-kaiser/.

12. Irving Wladawsky-Berger, "Data Science: From Half-Baked Ideas to Data-Driven Insights," CIO Journal, *The Wall Street Journal*, April 11, 2014, http://blogs.wsj.com/cio/2014/04/11/data-science-from-half-baked-ideas-to-data-driven-insights/.

13. Michael Hickins, "Fleet Management Co. to Sell Driving Data to Insurers," CIO Journal, *The Wall Street Journal*, March 12, 2014, http://blogs.wsj.com/cio/2014/03/12/fleet-management-co-to-sell-driving-data-to-insurers/.

14. Rachael King, "GM Grapples with Big Data, Cybersecurity in Vehicle Broadband Connections," CIO Journal, *The Wall Street Journal*, February 10, 2015, http://blogs.wsj.com/cio/2015/02/10/gm-grapples-with-big-data-cybersecurity-in-vehicle-broadband-connections/.

15. Steve Rosenbush, "Google's Ray Kurzweil Envisions New Era of Search," CIO Journal, *The Wall Street Journal*, February 4, 2014, http://blogs.wsj.com/cio/2014/02/04/googles-ray-kurzweil-envisions-new-era-of-search/.

16. Joshua Brustein, "Here are Alphabet's Most Notable Businesses Besides Google," Bloomberg Technology, August 10, 2015, https:// www.bloomberg.com/news/articles/2015-08-10/here-are-alphabet-s-most-notable-businesses-besides-google.

17. Steve Rosenbush, "Here's How Facebook Manages Big Data," CIO Journal, *The Wall Street Journal*, October 31, 2013, http://blogs. wsj.com/cio/2013/10/31/heres-how-facebook-manages-big-data/.

18. Tony Cosentino, "How Big Data Analytics Will Displace Net Promoter Score," Information Management, updated July 1, 2015, http://www.information-management.com/blogs/big-data-

analytics/Big-Data-Analytics-Net-Promoter-Score-Customer-Experience-10027194-1.html.

19. Bob Violino, "How Experian Is Using Big Data," Information Management, updated August 5, 2015, http://www.information-management.com/news/big-data-analytics/how-experian-is-using-big-data-10027341-1.html.

20. Rachael King, "How Intel's CIO Helped the Company Make $351 Million," CIO Journal, *The Wall Street Journal*, February 18, 2015, http://blogs.wsj.com/cio/2015/02/18/how-intels-cio-helped-the-company-make-351-million/.

21. Clint Boulton, "Intel Fighting Parkinson's Disease with Smartwatches, Big Data," CIO Journal, *The Wall Street Journal*, August 13, 2014, http://blogs.wsj.com/cio/2014/08/13/intel-fighting-parkinsons-disease-with-smartwatches-big-data/.

22. Rachael King, "Managing Moneyball Data," CIO Journal, *The Wall Street Journal*, September 26, 2013, http://blogs.wsj.com/cio/2013/09/26/managing-moneyball-data/.

23. Clint Boulton, "Michael Dell: The PC is Dell's Thin Edge of the Wedge," CIO Journal, *The Wall Street Journal*, May 30, 2014, http://blogs.wsj.com/cio/2014/05/30/michael-dell-the-pc-is-dells-thin-edge-of-the-wedge/.

24. Kim S. Nash, "Saks, Lord & Taylor Personalize Websites, Email to Lure High-Spending Shoppers," CIO Journal, *The Wall Street Journal*, July 7, 2015, http://blogs.wsj.com/cio/2015/07/07/saks-lord-taylor-personalize-websites-email-to-lure-high-spending-shoppers/.

25. Steven Norton, "Starwood Hotels Using Big Data to Boost Revenue," CIO Journal, *The Wall Street Journal*, February 10, 2015, http://blogs.wsj.com/cio/2015/02/10/starwood-hotels-using-big-data-to-boost-revenue/.

26. Steven Norton, "Time Inc. Pins Turnaround on Big Data, Specialty Content," CIO Journal, *The Wall Street Journal*, February 12, 2015, http://blogs.wsj.com/cio/2015/02/12/time-inc-pins-turnaround-on-big-data-specialty-content/.

27. Steve Rosenbush, "Visa Says Big Data Identifies Billions of Dollars in Fraud," March 11, 2013, http://blogs.wsj.com/cio/2013/03/11/visa-says-big-data-identifies-billions-of-dollars-in-fraud/.

28. Steve Rosenbush, "Air BnB Says Data is 'Lifeblood' of Fast-Growing Business," CIO Journal, *The Wall Street Journal*, March 20, 2014, http://blogs.wsj.com/cio/2014/03/20/airbnb-says-data-is-lifeblood-of-fast-growing-business/.

29. Ron Brooks, "Balancing Creative Data Monetization, Profits, and Customer Optics," Information Management, July 17, 2015, http://www.information-management.com/news/information-strategy-leadership/Data-Monetization-Strategies-Ethics-10027260-1.html.

30. Irving Wladawsky-Berger, "Better Living Through Data Science," CIO Journal, *The Wall Street Journal*, June 11, 2014, http://blogs.wsj.com/cio/2014/06/11/better-living-through-data-science-the-social-progress-index/.

31. Thomas H. Davenport, "Big Brown Finds Big Money from Big Data," CIO Journal, *The Wall Street Journal*, April 9, 2014, http://blogs.wsj.com/cio/2014/04/09/big-brown-finds-big-money-from-big-data/.

32. Seth Rosensweig, John Milani, Michael B. Flynn, "Big Data Banking Is Not Just for Big Banks," CIO Journal, *The Wall Street Journal*, May 27, 2014, http://blogs.wsj.com/cio/2014/05/27/big-data-banking-is-not-just-for-big-banks/.

33. Randy Bean, "Big Data and the Emergence of the Chief Data Officer," CIO Network, Forbes.com, August 8, 2016, http://

www.forbes.com/sites/ciocentral/2016/08/08/big-data-and-the-emergence-of-the-chief-data-officer/#493b250e6bb9.

34. Steven Norton, "Dickey's Barbecue Looks to Cloud for Edge Against Competitors Like Chipotle," CIO Journal, *The Wall Street Journal*, May 28, 2015, http://blogs.wsj.com/cio/2015/05/28/dickeys-barbecue-looks-to-cloud-for-edge-against-competitors-like-chipotle/.

35. Randy Bean, "Financial Services Companies Firms See Results from Big Data Push," CIO Journal, *The Wall Street Journal*, January 27, 2014, http://blogs.wsj.com/cio/2014/01/27/financial-services-companies-firms-see-results-from-big-data-push/.

36. Thomas H. Davenport, "Integrating Knowledge and Numbers," CIO Journal, *The Wall Street Journal*, April 16, 2014, http://blogs.wsj.com/cio/2014/04/16/integrating-knowledge-and-numbers/.

37. Thomas H. Davenport, "Lessons on Big Data Marketing," CIO Journal, *The Wall Street Journal*, May 14, 2014, http://blogs.wsj.com/cio/2014/05/14/lessons-on-big-data-marketing/.

38. Steve Rosenbush, "Property Firm Changes Business Model with Big Data," CIO Journal, *The Wall Street Journal*, http://blogs.wsj.com/cio/2014/02/10/property-firm-changes-business-model-with-big-data/.

39. Steve Rosenbush, "Property Firm Changes Business Model with Big Data," CIO Journal, *The Wall Street Journal*, February 10, 2014, http://blogs.wsj.com/cio/2014/02/10/property-firm-changes-business-model-with-big-data/.

40. Deloitte Insights, "Revitalize Core Systems for Strategic Growth," CIO Journal, *The Wall Street Journal*, May 13, 2015, http://deloitte.wsj.com/cio/2015/05/13/revitalize-core-systems-for-strategic-growth/.

41. Thomas H. Davenport, "Selling Analytics to Sales" CIO Journal, *The Wall Street Journal*, February 27, 2014, http://blogs.wsj.com/cio/2014/02/27/selling-analytics-to-sales/.

42. Kim S. Nash, "Tech Spin-off from Spice Maker McCormick Puts CIO in the CEO Seat," CIO Journal, *The Wall Street Journal*, April 1, 2015, http://blogs.wsj.com/cio/2015/04/01/tech-spin-off-from-spice-maker-mccormick-puts-cio-in-the-ceo-seat/.

43. Kim S. Nash, "Tech-Savvy Boards: Principal Financial Group CIO Consults Board on Strategic IT," CIO Journal, *The Wall Street Journal*, April 15, 2015, http://blogs.wsj.com/cio/2015/04/15/tech-savvy-boards-principal-financial-group-cio-consults-board-on-strategic-it/.

44. Thomas H. Davenport, "Telling Stories with Data," CIO Journal, *The Wall Street Journal*, June 12, 2013, http://blogs.wsj.com/cio/2013/06/12/telling-stories-with-data/.

45. Steve Rosenbush, "Twitter's Data Has Unique Value for Business," CIO Journal, *The Wall Street Journal*, November 7, 2013, http://blogs.wsj.com/cio/2013/11/07/twitters-data-has-unique-value-for-business/.

46. Mark J. Perry, "Fortune 500 Firms in 1955 vs. 2014; 88% are gone, and we're all better off because of that dynamic 'creative destruction,'" AEI Publications, last modified August 18, 2014, http://www.aei.org/publication/fortune-500-firms-in-1955-vs-2014-89-are-gone-and-were-all-better-off-because-of-that-dynamic-creative-destruction/.

Chapter 5: Data Strategy: Data Assets Are Better Than Data Liabilities

1. "Data As An Asset," blog entry by D. Justhy, December 11, 2015, http://data-as-an-asset.com/blogs/.

Chapter 6: How Data Intersects with Your Business Model and Business Strategy

1. Alexander Osterwalder, Yves Pigneur, *Business Model Generation: A Handbook*, (New York: Wiley, 2013.)

2. Jacque Bughin, Michael Chui, James Manyika, "Ten IT-Enabled Business Trends for the Decade Ahead," *McKinsey Quarterly*, May 2013, http://www.Mckinsey.com/industries/high-tech/our-insights/ten-it-enabled-business-trends-for-the-decade-ahead.

3. Dario Debarbieri, "Three Trends Businesses Should Embrace for a Digital Transformation," Forbes.com, March 7, 2016, http://www.forbes.com/sites/ibm/2016/03/07/three-trends-businesses-should-embrace-for-a-digital-transformation/#4fcc35e011b2.

4. "Infonomics," *Wikipedia*, last modified February 5, 2017, https://en.wikipedia.org/wiki/Infonomics.

5. Charles-Edouard Bouée, "Does Your Company Have a Plan D?" GE Reports, February 28, 2016, http://www.gereports.com/does-your-company-have-a-plan-d/.

Chapter 7: What the Life Cycle of Data Says About Your Enterprise

1. "The Fundamentals of data lifecycle management in the era of big data," (white paper, IBM Software, 2012), https://tdwi.org/~/media/E2658A46D24B4D9C88C782CDFB7B326B.PDF.

2. 2012 Global Reputational Risk and IT Study, IBM, 2012, https://www-935.ibm.com/services/us/gbs/bus/html/risk_study-2012-infographic.html.

Chapter 8: Going Digitally Global: The Right Way to Do It

1. "Beyond the Everyday Bank: How a GAFA Approach to Digital Banking Transformation Will Change Everything," white paper,

Accenture Consulting, 2016, https://www.accenture.com/us-en/insight-digital-banking-beyond-everyday-bank.

2. Gail Horwood, "Developing a Global Digital Strategy," Commentary, McKinsey & Company. October 2014, http://www.Mckinsey.com/business-functions/strategy-and-corporate-finance/our-insights/developing-a-global-digital-strategy.

3. James Manyika, Susan Lunch, Jacque Bughin, Jonathan Woetzel, Kalin Stamenov, Dhruv Dingra, "Digital globalization: The New Era of Global Flows," Report, McKinsey Global Institute, February 2016, http://www.Mckinsey.com/business-functions/digital-Mckinsey/our-insights/digital-globalization-the-new-era-of-global-flows.

4. Tanguy Catlin, Jay Scanlan, Paul Willmott, "Raising Your Digital Quotient," *McKinsey Quarterly*, June 2015, http://www.Mckinsey.com/business-functions/strategy-and-corporate-finance/our-insights/raising-your-digital-quotient.

5. Angus Dawson, Martin Hirt, Jan Scanlan, "The Economic Essentials of Digital Strategy," *McKinsey Quarterly*, March 2016, http://www.Mckinsey.com/business-functions/strategy-and-corporate-finance/our-insights/the-economic-essentials-of-digital-strategy.

6. "The Secrets to Going Digital: An Interview with Kate Smaje, by Barr Seitz, *McKinsey.com*, September 2015, http://www.Mckinsey.com/business-functions/organization/our-insights/the-secrets-to-going-digital.

7. Karel Dörner, David Edelman, "What 'Digital' Really Means," *McKinsey & Company,* July 2015, http://www.Mckinsey.com/industries/high-tech/our-insights/what-digital-really-means.

Chapter 9: Data Breaches and how to Avoid Them

1. The website of Ponemon Institute: ponemon.org, accessed February 12, 2017.
2. The website of *Infosecurity Magazine*: https://www.infosecurity-magazine.com, accessed February 12, 2017.
3. Fran Howarth, "The Damage of a Security Breach: Financial Institutions Face Monetary, Reputational Losses," *SecurityIntelligence*, April 30, 2015, https://securityintelligence.com/the-damage-of-a-security-breach-financial-institutions-face-monetary-reputational-losses/.
4. IBM 2015 Cyber Security Intelligence Index, IBM.com accessed February 12, 2017, http://www-01.ibm.com/common/ssi/cgi-bin/ssialias?htmlfid=SEW03073USEN.

Chapter 10: The DAAS Index: "Page Ranking" for Your Data

1. Lawrence Page, Sergey Brin, Rajeev Motwani, Terry Winograd, "The PageRank Citation Ranking: Bringing Order to the Web," *Stanford InfoLab Publication Server* (1999), http://ilpubs.stanford.edu:8090/422/.
2. The website of Clarity Square Technology: https//www.claritysquare.technology, accessed February 12, 2017

Chapter 11: Setting Up Your Team Members to Win with Data

1. Jack Welch, John A. Byrne, *Jack: Straight from the Gut*, (New York: Warner Business Books, 2003).
2. Jack Welch, Suzy Welch, *Winning*, (New York: Harper Business, 2005).

Chapter 12: How You Can Turn Big Data into Good Profits

1. Charles G. Koch, *Good Profit*, (New York: Crown Publishing, 2015).

2. Richard Ward, "A Billion-Dollar Opportunity for Oil Companies," *McKinsey & Company*, March 2016, http://www.Mckinsey. com/industries/oil-and-gas/our-insights/a-billion-dollar-digital-opportunity-for-oil-companies.

3. Nigel Shadbolt, Michael Chui, "Big Data, Big New Businesses," *Project Syndicate*, February 25, 2014, https://www.project-syndicate.org/commentary/nigel-shadbolt-and-michael-chui-estimate-that-the-annual-value-of-open-data-could-reach--3-trillion?barrier=accessreg.

4. Jörg Mayer, Marcus Schaper, "Data to Dollars: Supporting Top Management with Next-Generation Executive Information Systems," *McKinsey & Company*, January 2010, http://www. Mckinsey.com/business-functions/digital-Mckinsey/our-insights/ data-to-dollars-supporting-top-management-with-next-generation-executive-information-systems.

Morgan James
Speakers Group

www.TheMorganJamesSpeakersGroup.com

We connect Morgan James published
authors with live and online events
and audiences whom will benefit
from their expertise.